THE *Feisty* FREELANCER

THE *Feisty* FREELANCER

A Friendly Guide to Visioning, Planning, and Growing Your Writing Business

SUZANNE BOWNESS

DUNDURN PRESS

Copyright © Suzanne Bowness, 2025
Editorial cartoons © Iva Cheung (CC BY-NC), ivacheung.com

All rights reserved. No part of this publication may be reproduced, stored in a retrieval system, or transmitted in any form or by any means, electronic, mechanical, photocopying, recording, or otherwise (except for brief passages for purpose of review) without the prior permission of Dundurn Press. Permission to photocopy should be requested from Access Copyright.

Publisher: Meghan Macdonald | Acquiring editor: Kathryn Lane | Editor: Robyn So
Cover designer: Karen Alexiou
Cover image: typewriter: mhatzapa/istock.com; highlighter lines: Hanna Siamashka /istock.com

Library and Archives Canada Cataloguing in Publication

Title: The feisty freelancer : a friendly guide to visioning, planning, and growing your writing business / Suzanne Bowness.
Names: Bowness, Suzanne, 1976- author
Description: Includes index.
Identifiers: Canadiana (print) 20240456750 | Canadiana (ebook) 20240456793 | ISBN 9781459755017 (softcover) | ISBN 9781459755024 (PDF) | ISBN 9781459755031 (EPUB)
Subjects: LCSH: Authorship—Vocational guidance.
Classification: LCC PN151 .B69 2025 | DDC 808.02—dc23

We acknowledge the support of the Canada Council for the Arts and the Ontario Arts Council for our publishing program. We also acknowledge the financial support of the Government of Ontario, through the Ontario Book Publishing Tax Credit and Ontario Creates, and the Government of Canada.

Care has been taken to trace the ownership of copyright material used in this book. The author and the publisher welcome any information enabling them to rectify any references or credits in subsequent editions.

The publisher is not responsible for websites or their content unless they are owned by the publisher.

Printed and bound in Canada.

Dundurn Press
1382 Queen Street East
Toronto, Ontario, Canada M4L 1C9
dundurn.com, @dundurnpress

*Dedicated to all the feisty freelancers out there,
working independently together*

Contents

Introduction: What's Your Freelance Story?	1
1: The Coolest Way You'll Ever Work (Maybe?)	11
2: Getting Down to Business	23
3: Just the Business Basics, Baby	45
4: Reading Like a Writer	63
5: The Art of the Pitch	75
6: How to Write an Article	87
7: Pitching Corporate Clients	103
8: Collaborating with Editors and Clients	119
9: Productivity 101	133
10: Pricing Services, Getting Paid	143
11: Marketing Your Business	165
12: Staying Motivated While Working from Home	179
13: Advancement Strategies for Successful Freelancers	193
14: AI and the Future of Freelancing	205
Conclusion: On Your Way	215
Acknowledgements	217
Appendix A: Resources for Writers	219
Appendix B: A Q&A Chorus of Other Voices	223

Index 273

About the Author 277

Introduction

What's Your Freelance Story?

Welcome to *The Feisty Freelancer*. I'm writing this at 9:30 p.m. on a Tuesday, after goofing off yesterday. I visited the CNE (Canadian National Exhibition) in Toronto with my mother, who lives in a different city. Neither of us is much for roller coasters, so we spent the afternoon looking around the international craft pavilion, watching an ice dancing show, and trying out the Ferris wheel because it's the only midway ride we can handle. Now it's the day after, and tonight I'm working late to catch up on some writing projects so I'll be able to meet my deadlines this week.

While yesterday I spent no hours at work and today I've spent too many hours at work, these two days represent one of my favourite aspects of freelancing: the fact that I decide how I spend my hours, weeks, and months. Mind you, while I was at the CNE, I did check my smartphone several times to field clients' emails about current projects. I also can't play hooky every day, or I'd have no clients. But this is my fun. The activities may change — occasional Friday afternoon matinees are a favourite — but the freedom to drop fun breaks into my working life is a treat that I relish and my friends envy. I am a freelancer.

As a writer/editor who has spent most of my twenty-plus-years career freelancing, I chose this self-employment pathway because of this freedom, not only in terms of my schedule but also in terms of choosing my projects and steering my overall career. If I get bored of a niche, I transition to a new one. If a client proves difficult, I fire them. If I want to take a month off to try living in New York City or being a tourist in England, I do, with careful planning. If I need to earn an extra $500 a month, I sit down and seriously think about how I can pitch enough billable work to get there. I love not having to ask a boss for the morning off for a dental appointment, or to take a longer lunch, or to start work an hour later because I'm an occasional insomniac who needs her sleep to do focused work. I take long holidays most summers (strategically, when most of my clients are away) and often work that little week between Christmas and New Year's because I get a lot done in that quiet time (people call it Q5, as in the secret extra quarter of the year, and now I do too!). A lot of these lifestyle benefits became more apparent to office workers who were thrown into working from home by the misfortune of the Covid-19 pandemic. They newly revel in being able to wear leggings and put on a load of laundry in the middle of the day. To which I say, SEE? THIS IS WHAT I'VE BEEN TALKING ABOUT ALL ALONG!

My Story

My personal entry into freelancing started on a sad day as I walked with tears rolling down my face, carrying my box of desk decor and other personal items in a brown cardboard box. At age twenty-five, I didn't even know a person could be laid off, or magazines could fold, or creative work could be brought to a grinding halt, to use a cliché. I'd been let go from my first editorial job, along with our entire staff of over twenty-five people.

But in the days after that low moment, as I began to contemplate next steps, I thought back to a group of workers I had observed from my cubicle at the magazine. These shadow figures seemed central to our operation, yet just as free to peddle their bylines to other magazines before bouncing back to us again. They'd show up at our offices to meet with a senior editor, then disappear again into the daylight, their byline a few weeks or months later the only trace that they'd even been there.

My main task in my role as online editor at the magazine (*Saturday Night*, Rest In Peace until you are resurrected again) was to figure out fun, audience-growing ways to translate the magazine online, and so my major contact with freelancers was to invite their pitches on how to extend their articles online and to solicit extra content they produced while writing the article (online photo outtakes? interview transcripts? Q&As?).

Sometimes the freelancers would also ask for extra money for these transcripts and outtakes. "Do we have a budget?" I'd ask my supervisor. Sometimes, to my surprise, we did.

I was impressed with the freelancers who asked regardless, because they demanded to be paid for the extra rather than just giving it away. I would later learn that not every freelancer has this confidence, but I admired it where I saw it. I was also enamoured with their lifestyle and creative ownership. While we were all putting in long hours on the cubicle farm, freelancers were the ones credited with the stories. They did everything from interviewing celebrities to investigating complex issues and translating them for the average reader, raising awareness, and sometimes even changing minds on important issues.

Even though I loved my online editor role, I had already filed this new job title "freelancer" away in the back of my mind. I figured that maybe in ten years I'd look into it, after learning the ropes at my favourite magazine, adding a few more articles to the two front-of-book pieces I'd already written for the magazine, maybe ascending to associate and then senior editor, and figuring out what an editorial career looked like for me.

A Writer from Early On

In terms of overall career, I also knew from way back that I wanted to be mostly writing. I'm lucky to be one of those humans who knew from an early age what she wanted to be when she grew up. While everyone was saying astronaut, I was saying writer. I was a huge reader as a kid, and authors like Gordon Korman, Lucy Maud Montgomery, and Lois Lowry were my heroes. As I grew older, I came to realize that you also needed to figure out how to make a living. Pondering the inroads into fiction and learning the hard truth that nobody was going to pay me to write my first novel, I started to see non-fiction equally as a way to put words together and to tell stories — and get paid for it from day one.

I validated this interest by writing a column about my high school for the local community newspaper. Then I became editor of my university college newspaper, confirming further that I liked journalism and creating publications. After failing my first round of full-time internship applications in the summer after graduating from university, I found three part-time jobs and squeezed in a part-time volunteer internship at a music magazine (whenever I hear one-hit wonder Len's "Steal My Sunshine" it brings me right back to that summer). Then, finally, I secured an internship at *Saturday Night* for the fall, using my (not really) wizard skills in HTML that I'd taught myself as a way to stave off boredom in one of my part-time jobs in university.

That internship extended into my dream first job as the magazine's first online editor, which turned into my nightmare layoff. But as I tasted the world of magazine work and found myself already supervising an assistant editor and a handful of interns, I had to admit I wasn't writing as much as I thought I'd be. Could the silver lining of the layoff be to work my way back to my first love? While the timeline was earlier than expected, I thought freelancing might be the best route to a fuller embrace of writing.

I took myself out of the traditional job pathway and found a way to work that suits my independent, curiosity-driven personality. Mine in particular is a pathway that involves non-fiction writing and mostly a mix of journalism and corporate work that looks like journalism, along with some copy editing and proofreading that fills out the last quarter to a third of my time. Although I've been freelancing full-time for twenty-plus years, I have also, particularly in the early days, taken on three-ish-month contracts part-time, from working as a proofreader on launches of new *Globe and Mail* websites to working at a couple of creative agencies, always keeping up my freelancing alongside those gigs. I've also been teaching writing courses since 2004, one or two per term, at various colleges and universities. In this book, when I mention my students, I'm talking about the legion of writing students that I've taught over the years, mostly in the Professional Writing and Communications graduate certificate program that I helped to develop at Humber College. I now cheer these students on via LinkedIn and other platforms. All of this to say that even with full-time freelancing, you can dip in and out or try new things, make them part-time, or take on a side hustle. If the flexibility is one of the biggest perks, take advantage of this perk in every way.

Despite the challenges (see: feast-famine cycle) I have been a relatively happy freelancer, and the flexibility it has afforded me has brought a lot to my life (see: Friday afternoon matinees). If you are thinking freelancing might be for you, please read on. If you're on the fence, still read on to get a sense of what this life is really like. If you're deeply suspicious of freelancing, feel free to get a fantastic traditional editorial job where you treat freelancers really nicely, and we'll try to make you look smart for hiring us.

Your Story?

Freelancing is not for everyone. And it doesn't have to be full-time. But unfortunately, in today's up-and-down economy, many writers and editors will consider it as an option at one point or another. While the selling points of a career as an editorial freelancer are the creativity, the variety, and the fact that if you're serious and getting enough contracts to work full-time you can actually carve out a decent living, anyone who says it is a straightforward and stable path has probably not met many freelancers. The good news is that freelancing is indeed a decent side hustle to an editorial career, a filler for the (more than) occasional employment gap that the average writer experiences and, for some of us, can be the bulk of a satisfying creative career.

Even if you never freelance, I hope that reading about the freelance mindset makes you think more entrepreneurially about your traditional editorial career. What could you accomplish if you think more like a freelancer? Could you pitch your corporate boss on the project you'd really like to work on rather than the boring project she tasked you with? Could you advocate for 20 percent free time, which it's rumoured some Googlers have, to work on your own projects? Even if you're not a freelancer, feel free to borrow our feisty.

But in truth, this book is really for those who are seriously considering taking up the freelance identity in the longer term, either full-time or part-time. And it's equally for those who are early in their editorial career (I always advise working for a few years in a traditional workplace for the learning and mentorship) or those making the transition later on in their career. To decide if freelancing is for you, I think there are some questions you need to ask yourself. In the next chapter, I'll walk you through a few of these questions (not wanting to scare you off quite yet), but in short, you need to be self-disciplined, fine with working in relative solitude, and also okay with reaching out to find your projects rather than having them filtered to you through a supervisor. That's not to say you need to be an extrovert; I would say I am Captain Introvert and I still manage to keep myself employed. The outreach is not my favourite part of the work, but the rest is sufficient payoff to make me keep at it.

If you are keen on trying out life as a freelancer, I want you to have the best shot at it and maybe skip some of the mistakes I made when I didn't know things or was afraid to ask. In this book, which originated as a shorter e-book for students in a course I taught on freelancing, I cover the basics of setting up a business, how to pitch both publications and corporate clients, how to develop good editorial relationships, how to price your services and get paid, how to create a work-from-home space that you actually want to sit in for eight hours a day (with breaks), and even a few thoughts on how to keep things interesting when you're a grizzled old-timer like me. Plus thoughts on the future of our industry (to be taken with a large grain of salt). At the end of the book, I also include a handful of interviews with other freelancers to expand the viewpoint beyond my own.

Furthermore, to gain a perspective beyond my own around financial topics such as pricing and retirement, I created a short, unscientific survey of freelancers and posted it on various writer/editor listservs and social media platforms. The survey was anonymous. I've sprinkled the results throughout the book. Let me tell you about this generous group of sixty Canadian freelancers:

- 68 percent freelance full-time versus 32 percent part-time
- 83 percent are female, 16 percent are male, 1 percent are non-binary
- 52 percent are from Central Canada, 32 percent are from Eastern Canada, and 14 percent from Western Canada
- the vast majority of respondents are over age 35

Of course, editorial freelancing encompasses many other areas. I have friends who work on internal communications, writing emails and other correspondence. Some writers work mainly on grants, raising money for non-profits and other deserving organizations. As social media has grown, many freelancers focus on that niche, creating posts and plans and even specializing in specific platforms. I know many freelancers whose business is mostly editing, with a focus on niches from magazines to academic editing to book editing. The results of my freelancer survey showed that participants provided writing services and editing services about equally. Somewhat fewer participants also provide proofreading services, while others listed social media content, grant writing, research, translation, graphic design, coaching/training, project management, and indexing among their services.

Regardless of your focus, what most editorial freelancers have in common is that they typically value the freelance lifestyle, and they are always looking out for new opportunities, developing client relationships, and doing work that surpasses expectations so they get called on over and over again. Freelancers are usually entrepreneurial, although I've met freelancers who don't particularly think of themselves as being in business so much as they think of themselves as independent workers. And vice versa, there's those who shrug off the freelance title in favour of business owner. I think the tent is big enough for all of us.

While I choose (and celebrate) this lifestyle every day for the freedom and variety, it's still work. Not work would be watching Netflix all day, which would be fun too, although probably not great support for other goals like continuing to eat and pay rent. Some people try to act as if self-employment is a breeze, and while I find it fun, there's a lot that goes into making it work. And the time that's required is fairly comparable to a standard work week (sorry, Timothy Ferriss — I'm just not sold on your four-hour work week). I even keep nine-to-five hours that mirror those of the business world, since I figure that's when my editors are in the office (and I get too much FOMO, or fear of missing out, when I work too far into the evening and think of everyone off having drinks on the patio without me). But as long as you put the hours in at some point, then you're fine. Work-life balance is a funny concept, because often it's not a daily balance but more that your life is working in balance most of the time despite some off-balance days and weeks. A freelance lifestyle means that if you need the morning to take your cat to the vet, then sometimes you work in the evening to make up the time. Swap in "take your kid on the field trip" and "work after bedtime," or "take elderly parent to doctor's appointment" and "work after you get home or early in the morning (ugh)" as needed here.

Okay, so I acted cool about freelancers who think of themselves as independent workers, but I really think if you're going to do it long-term, it's helpful to think of yourself as a business — someone who is in this not only for the creative opportunity but also for the money. To decide how much you want to earn alongside other goals, set your intended salary as a target. Resiliency, tenacity, persistence — I've chosen FEISTY — all are good qualities in a freelancer.

Just a few notes about who should be reading this book: it's mostly geared to editorial freelancers, but feel free to lend it to your designer colleague or your illustrator friend, or even to your lawyer acquaintance starting out as a solo, as many notes apply equally to many other creative business owners. Have these colleagues drop me a note if they would like their own feisty guide to starting a business in their niche, and I'll pass it along to my publisher. ☺

This book is also geared to the junior writer/editor who decides to go freelance early in their career like I did and to the experienced mid- or late-career writer or communications professional who has decided to try this fun, new working style. The latter may want to skip over some parts where I cover basic skills, although even as an experienced writer I'm always curious about how others do things, so feel free to dive in. I also speak mostly about writing, but the advice is equally for other editorial freelancers with a focus on editing and other specialties.

Finally, this book is geared mostly toward freelancing in Canada, with Canadian examples in the more technical details, like taxes and business set-up. But I hope that freelancers in other countries, including our big neighbour to the south, will also benefit and can just look up the equivalent rules in their areas. Also, just a reminder — I will mention it again directly where applicable — that anywhere I give advice that seems remotely legal or financial, I am not an expert, so please check with your own specialists.

So, let's get on with it. In the chapters to follow, I'm going to pass on not only the fundamentals I learned in my start-up but also everything I've learned in the interim that's specific to freelancing and to writing/editing in particular. At the end of most chapters, I've included some exercises to prompt further thinking and action. Where I don't end with exercises, I include a fun cartoon from editor Iva Cheung to keep a smile on your face. All freelancers start in different ways, and I hope that by reading this book and sampling the exercises you will begin your journey into what I think is a fun, and sometimes even lucrative, adventure.

Chapter 1

The Coolest Way You'll Ever Work (Maybe?)

Although I've alluded to the fabulous free-range lifestyle of the freelance writer, you may still be wondering, *What exactly does the job involve? How is this work the same and different from a regular writer/editor staff job? Is there an application form to be a freelancer?*

Funny, I just looked up "freelancing" in the second edition of the *Canadian Oxford Dictionary*, our dictionary of record in Canada, and I already disagree slightly with its definition of "a person offering services on a temporary basis." Not my freelancing, honey. I think the Wikipedia definition of "a person who is self-employed and not necessarily committed to a particular employer long-term" (last edited March 2, 2024) or the *Merriam-Webster Dictionary*'s version of "a person who pursues a profession without a long-term commitment to any one employer" (accessed May 19, 2024) work better, although they don't fully address the entrepreneurship angle. These definitions make freelancers seem like uncommitted in-betweens, as opposed to a generation of feisty entrepreneurs whose company I am proud to keep. Maybe I didn't set out to embrace this way of life, but I do now.

The Work

So, no, there's no application form, and freelancer as a title is self-declared. Some people won't call themselves freelancers because the title of "consultant" is preferred in their industries. I also call myself a consultant on my business website, and I'm choosy about using the word "freelancer" when reaching out to corporate clients (magazine editors are familiar with the term, and it might seem pretentious to use other titles in the journalism world). Many freelancers, including me, equally embrace an identity as self-employed or business owners. Given the definitions of freelancer above, you can see there's a bit of bias against the term. But regardless of title, freelancers do have quite a bit in common with each other and with staff writers and editors. Like those on staff, we spend our days working on writing and editing assignments large and small, dealing with supervisors (in the case of freelancers, with clients), and developing ideas for future projects.

Freelancers do research, we interview (especially we journalist types), we outline, draft, write, edit. Freelance editors take on texts of all varieties, from books to reports, and improve everything from organization to grammar. Then we editorial freelancers also do a bunch of business stuff that our in-house colleagues have no idea about: pitching, following up on pitches or client requests, following up on the follow-ups. We invoice and track our payments and our monthly income. We learn about new tools that could help in our business or new forms that seem to be coming into the marketplace (hello Facebook, then Snapchat, then Instagram, then TikTok). We do activities to increase our visibility, such as attending networking events or interacting on social platforms. Many of these business tasks are common to all creative businesses, and they're the extra we do to keep our names top of mind for assignments and, in a broader sense, the privilege of working independently. Sometimes we hire people to do tasks where our time is better spent on our core skills (see: accounting).

Besides the common business tasks, probably the biggest difference for freelancers is the regular outreach for work to both editors at publications and new corporate clients to pitch ideas or our expertise as writers. We are also the chief cooks and bottle washers, as the expression goes, acting as our own IT departments, contract negotiators, and buyers of office supplies.

Clients contract work to freelancers for several reasons: they are understaffed, either permanently or during busy periods; they fall in love with a fabulous idea that the freelancer has pitched (as a reward for our cleverness we get to write the thing); and they build a business model around outsourcing a portion of their work. Freelance editors are in demand both by organizations that focus on texts as their main output, such as publishers, and also by organizations that handle writing internally but know that their output would be greatly enhanced by the grammatical eyes of a professional (these organizations are correct). Being available and open to opportunities when clients call and having a constant eye out for new stories or ideas to pitch are two ways to stay in good favour with your clients and develop a thriving enterprise.

The Perks

I already reviewed the perks of freelancing in the introduction, but they bear repeating. Top among them are flexibility and the control you get over your life: time for family, time for hobbies, the ability to schedule your workload according to your energy levels instead of some supervisor's idea of when things should get done. If you don't believe me, check out the Q&As at the end of this book, where this perk is cited again and again. As long as you fit the work in and make time for it, the how and where it gets done matter less. In fact, it's been interesting to see the office work-from-home movement grow post-pandemic, where people who work in traditional jobs are pushing back against re-entering the workplace full-time because it's hard to give up those perks once you have them (see: entire freelance career).

I have to admit, I'm a bit jealous that benefits I've earned by the extra effort of self-employment have just been handed to a swath of work-from-home employees who still get to earn their regular salaries. But at the same time, being your own boss means you don't need to manage an employer, as I think of it.

Another element of freelancing that I enjoy is the variety of work you can take on and the ability to choose your projects. I am somewhat indecisive, so when I think of my dream job, a lot of different organizations come to mind. The good news is that I've been able to work for many of these organizations and yet still build something of my own. I may complain about the universal work-from-home opportunity but, in fact, I earn more as a freelancer than I might at some (not all) senior-level editorial jobs, and when you add up the perks, my own pendulum has definitely swung in favour of self-employment. Yet another upside is that the cost of entry to this business is relatively low, requiring just your trusty laptop and a good internet connection (and a few more items, but not nearly the same upfront costs as a retail store with inventory).

The Challenges

You'll notice that I didn't get into the challenges of freelancing in the introduction because I didn't want to scare you away immediately. But you've probably heard about the challenges already. The main one is financial instability or, perhaps more specifically, financial unpredictability. I have a nickname for this: July. Most years in the month of July, I make at least one panicked phone call to my mother in which I tell her that I have absolutely no work that week and really don't know what I'll do as I watch my emergency fund fall lower and the crickets chirp outside my window. Every year, her answer is "You've been doing this work for X years. You've paid your rent and gone on great vacations and managed to keep your cats in kibble, so why don't you just relax and refresh your website or one of those other things you're always saying you'll get to just as soon as things ease up a bit?" (Aren't moms great?)

And she's right. Inevitably a client calls and workdays slide into productivity again. I've also learned to take my vacations in July so the month doesn't feel as stark. On the opposite end of this equation, you'll have months that are just swamped (hello, September). Freelancers often refer to this as the feast or famine cycle. So that's a thing, and some are better at mitigating it than others, and some niches are more protected from it than others. If you can't live with that uncertainty (or you have people who depend on you who can't live with it), then freelance may not be for you. Working on 100 percent commission is challenging. Also, you'll miss other work perks like health benefits and pensions, so you have to figure out a way to self-fund those pesky necessities. I'll discuss these icky financial topics a bit more in the next chapter when I touch on goal-setting as a freelancer.

Another challenge is one I alluded to earlier: you need to be self-directed and good at time management, plus assertive enough to pick up the phone or send out emails asking for work. If you don't reach out, you won't get projects, and if you aren't good at time management, you won't meet your deadlines (then you'll lose the work). All that management takes organization, a decent scheduling tool, and motivation.

The routine of rejection is another hardship. Even a skilled and experienced freelancer can encounter it, and as a junior it's even more crushing because you don't yet have the writing samples or client base. My most hated form of rejection is what I call the "wall of silence," where people just don't get back to you. But even with my preferred variety of rejection, where you reach a sympathetic editor who is apologetic and encouraging, the reasons for a negative response can border on the absurd. A few years ago, I pitched a short article about chickens being bred to preserve their heritage bloodlines and essentially adopted by donors in exchange for naming rights and a dozen eggs every two weeks. When I approached a national general interest magazine, the editor's rejection was based on the fact that the magazine "had already done another chicken story in the past few months." I replied that I supposed I would have to abandon my specialty in chicken stories (not a niche), but I'm not sure the editor grasped my attempt at wit. My point here is that even after years of freelancing, I still experience rejection on a regular basis. I suppose that's in part because I pitch a lot and therefore leave myself open (the acceptances are worth it). So, you have to train yourself not to take it personally. And to move on quickly.

Yet another downside is that people, including your family, will resist understanding what you do and may even ask repeatedly when you plan to get a real job. In the workplace, as an outside contractor you have no visibility, you're not in the cubicle down the hall or even in the internal email address book. So, you have to work harder to get noticed or remembered for your contributions. There's no standard corporate ladder as a freelancer, so some workplaces may be reluctant to outsource more strategic senior-level work that you might have been assigned if you had the equivalent role internally. They may take a while even to trust you with a bigger project initially, and you may need to start with more junior assignments and prove yourself to each new client unless you came in with a strong referral. However, there are ways to keep your work interesting and pursue more senior opportunities, as I cover in a later chapter. Plus, you can take your lunch break whenever you damn well please.

Before I talk you out of this whole gig, I'm going to reiterate the fun aspects: control over your schedule, being your own boss, choosing your projects, working in your pyjamas (that's a bit of a stereotype — I definitely dress as though I was going to leave the house every day). There's also the flipside of the elements I just mentioned: while you may be a bit more isolated, you also avoid that whole mess known as office politics. I also find I'm a lot more productive when I'm able to skip the endless meetings I hear are required at many workplaces and organize my own schedule instead of waiting for instructions from a supervisor.

I'm going to assume that if you've read this far you just might read the whole darn text to find out why I have any enthusiasm for this way of life despite its challenges. So, let's dive in.

Taking the Plunge

I started my business by taking an eight-week self-employment program that I qualified for through a Canadian-government Employment Insurance program after my layoff. My version was called the Self-Employment Assistance program; the name has changed over the years, and it is currently shelved, although I hope they bring it back, because I have met so many people over the years who benefitted from it (high fives to all the SEA grads out there!). Participants in the program learned business basics, from doing market research to creating a business plan to learning how to create an invoice. In this particular program, they admitted a variety of businesses, and our class of approximately thirty included a restaurateur, a reiki therapist, a computer technician, a fashion designer, and a dating coach, just to name a few. Many are still in business (the restaurateur, who maxed out several credit cards to start his operation after he was denied a business loan, is doing particularly well. I smile every time I walk by his restaurant in downtown Toronto).

While we were all different, we all had entrepreneurship in common, and I think that is one of the most recognizable characteristics of the successful freelancer. That goes doubly for a career freelancer, who not only writes a few stories but also tries to build a business that will earn repeat clientele and a long-standing reputation. If you're looking for ways into freelancing, you can start by reading books like this one (or one of the others that I list in the resources list at the end of this book). For those who are new to writing altogether or want to reskill in a different form (social media?) there are individual writing courses you can take or whole college and university programs that provide you with a year or two of training plus an internship to help you get some experience.

I actually started my writing career by applying for internships and taking one as on-the-job training right out of my undergraduate degree in literary studies (like English but studying works in translation alongside the canon) and history, although I sort of wish I had taken a writing program (fewer were available then), so I would've known the basics already.

You can take courses and workshops on how to set up your business; try out freelancing part-time on top of your other work, whether writing or not; or take a sabbatical if you have a flexible job. If you're thinking seriously about freelancing full-time, try taking a month off and following some of the approaches suggested in this book to see whether it works for you on that longer-term basis. Don't worry, I'll wait.

So, how was it? Whether it's the month-long trial or a full leap of faith, the only way to confirm that the freelance life going to work for you is to try it. Even if you're not sure, the good news is that it's not one of those paths where you have to go all in at first pitch. In fact, if you have a full-time job, I'd probably keep it and start by trying to make room for some freelance projects on the side. If you're the type who likes to jump in feet first (or if a layoff gives you a push like it did for me), I'd suggest you have six months to a year of savings in the bank to cover your rent and expenses so you can feel more comfortable as you give it a shot. Marrying rich, finding a patron, taking a leave from an existing job, or having a parent or uncle who owns a major media empire are also recommended. But most powerfully, a love of writing and the persistence to keep at it despite rejection will be your best assets.

To assist you in further understanding the job of a freelancer, I thought it might be helpful to break it down by day, month, and year. Remember, these schedules are reflective of my life as a non-fiction journalist and content writer, which may differ from other types of freelancing, although I suspect that most elements will be similar.

A Day in the Life

As I mentioned, I'm a nine-to-fiver, meaning I'm at my desk by 9:00 a.m. and try to look up by 5:00 p.m. to see if I'm able to quit for the day. I keep these hours to match those of most office workers at their desks, including editors, since it's easiest to reach most working people at this time for everything from phone interviews to pitches (two regular items on my daily to-do list).

Others action items include answering emails from public relations (PR) contacts, researching new story ideas, sending introductory emails to prospective clients, catching up with established clients, and posting on social media, plus the actual bread-and-butter tasks of writing and editing. Deadlines often drive the order of these activities, so a deadline day will see me mostly writing, while on other days my activities are more mixed.

A Week in the Life

At the start of a typical week, I generally look at my assignment deadlines and plan my week around meeting them. At the same time, I know I won't have assignments for the next week(s) if I don't continue to do some prospecting, so I also try to plan some outreach activities, whether it be reaching out to a couple of editors, researching and developing some pitches, or checking in with a corporate client or two.

There are also business administrative tasks, like sending invoices, updating my website and social platforms, and reading publications I'd like to pitch. I try to keep an eye on these tasks on a weekly basis, with a check-in at the end of the month to make sure I'm on track.

A Year in the Life

I have always loved New Year's resolutions! Every year I take a day or two to reflect on new goals for my business. Are there any new clients or niches I want to pursue? Is my work-life balance where I want it to be? Is it time to give myself a cost-of-living raise, either in my hourly rate or in the per-word rate I charge to publications? I look over what efforts from the past year yielded the best results, what I need to give more attention to going forward, and what new technologies and story forms have emerged that I may need to learn. I even think about what I should drop because I'm not enjoying it or it's not profitable — for example, discontinuing my efforts on a social media platform that isn't bringing any return.

I try to pick two or three elements to pursue and track for the year, and I keep an eye on these goals moving forward. I also reflect on my income goals and create a new spreadsheet to track income and expenses monthly. Then I try to schedule time for all my new activities and plan to check in mid-year (back-to-school-era resolutions are my second-favourite kind).

So? Ready to give freelancing a try? What do you have to lose? Let's start a business. Or maybe you want to try the exercises at the end of the chapter first. If your results strengthen your resolve, join me in chapter 2.

Exercises

EXERCISE 1

Is freelancing right for you? Here are some questions you should think about before starting on this path. As you read through them, try to think of some examples from your personal or professional life, where you demonstrated those skills.

- Do you have the self-discipline to set up and maintain a regular workday routine without the motivation of a supervisor?
- Are you a self-starter who is always reading and looking for story ideas?
- Are your writing and editing skills at the level where you can get work professionally, or are you committed to developing and upgrading your skills to be competitive?
- Are you good at time management?
- Can you (and your partner and dependents) handle financial ups and downs? Are you willing to self-fund benefits and plan for your own retirement without a pension?
- Are you amenable to managing all of the tasks involved in running a business, not only writing and editing, but invoicing, record-keeping, and tax saving?
- Are you okay with cold calling, networking, and other initially icky salesy elements?

EXERCISE 2

Consider the freelance pros and cons. Of the pros, which one excites you the most? Of the cons, which one scares you the most? Are there any ways you can plan to address those fears from the start?

Chapter 2

Getting Down to Business

Welcome to Day One of your freelance writing business. Congratulations on taking the plunge! Uh, now what? Before you lift a finger to the keyboard, you'll have to figure out a few things about the kind of business you want to run and put yourself into the mindset of a business owner. After all, good or bad, work is no longer going to flow to you from some overworked supervisor. You have to make it happen.

If the upside to total freedom is … total freedom … the downside is … total freedom. That means nobody tells you what time to be at work. Nobody reminds you to invoice for your work. Nobody tells you to pay your taxes. (Well, the government does … eventually. By then you're in trouble.) So, you need to think about all the elements both creative and practical that go into setting up a business. Fortunately, you're already reading this book. Don't worry, I've got ya.

While some people find embracing the title of business owner a challenge, others find even calling themselves a writer feels like a stretch. I've never had this problem, probably because I've wanted to be a writer since grade 3, but so many of my writing students have told me that they have had trouble overcoming impostor syndrome, even after writing many pieces and receiving much feedback on their talents. If you truly are weak in some areas, then find training and resources to improve. If you're getting good feedback on your writing already, if you're the one that your friends come to for editing advice, then I think my only advice here is fake it until you make it. Keep writing and editing so that you strengthen your skills, and maybe don't overthink it so much — if you're writing and people are publishing your writing willingly, then you appear to be a writer!

Same thing with being a business owner. Embrace it. Eventually, it will feel more natural.

Now that your mindset is rock-solid (ha), it's time to think about the specifics. How will you approach the whole writing-business project? "Branding" is a bit of a buzzword, but I think it's a great way of describing the ways in which you create a persona for yourself and your business. It also helps you to gain focus, particularly in those early days when you are figuring out the industry and making your first inroads.

Thankfully, your major decision has already been made — you're going to provide editorial services. But even that focus area represents a broad range: writers produce everything from brochures to white papers to tweets. Editors niche into academic editing, book editing, and more. What do you like to do?

If you like to write mostly journalistic articles, maybe you'll want to gear your business toward publications. But as a freelancer looking to make a good living, you'll likely want to spend at least some of your time producing editorial materials for organizations other than publishers as well — not only do they generally pay better, but there are also more companies out there than publications.

Here is a sample of writing forms you may be asked to tackle as a freelancer:

- Newsletter articles — articles that cover everything from news to profiles, usually short, combined with other articles, and issued monthly or weekly
- Media releases — also called "press release" or "news release" — a one-page, very templated form used to announce a new development or product or event, issued by companies in the hopes that journalists write about the topic
- Website pages — copy for a "landing page" (home page) plus other pages on a website, such as About, Contact, etc.
- Social media content (tweets, reels, Facebook posts) — see your favourite platform
- Emails — companies hire writers to create emails that do everything from connecting with their audiences to selling products; sometimes emails are written in sequences for sales purposes
- Internal reports, memos, and emails — despite being distributed internally, many company communications are drafted by outside providers
- Fundraising letters — highly templated letters that use storytelling and calls-to-action to convince people to donate money
- Brochures — usually an 8.5- x 11-inch page folded in three with a set format; they are used to sell or advertise
- Sell sheets — typically a one-page, double-sided copy used to help corporate salespeople capture the essence of a product they want to sell; sell sheets are used regularly in the tech world
- Proposals — used by everyone from businesses to arts organizations — help to define an idea and are

often used to convince the reader to fund or start a project
- Training manuals — one of several forms of technical writing, training manuals break down a process step by step so that a person can follow the instructions to accomplish a task
- Executive biographies — biographies of key people in an organization, often developed for companies with a formal structure/hierarchy or with a lot of employees
- Annual reports — a document that pulls together success stories from the past year at a company as well as financial reports to provide insight into a company's progress
- Speeches — written for oral delivery, a text that captures a speaker's voice, usually written for a specific event or occasion
- Case studies — a sales tool that uses storytelling to show how a product or service improved a client's life or business; they're often used in technology or business-to-business communications
- White papers — a long-form essay used in the technology industry to explain a complex application for the purpose of helping a decision-maker understand a product

You'll also be asked to edit documents beyond just catching typos. Here are the different stages of editing that a document might need, as defined by the national professional association Editors Canada, which has established a set of Professional Editorial Standards and professional certification exams. The standards were updated in 2024 and can be downloaded for free from the Editors Canada website (editors.ca).

- Structural editing — assessing and shaping the overall organization and content of the material to optimize it for the intended audience, medium, and purpose (also called substantive editing)
- Stylistic editing — clarifying meaning, ensuring coherence and flow at the paragraph and sentence level, and refining the language
- Copy editing — reviewing material to ensure correct and consistent grammar, punctuation, spelling, and usage; it often includes checking that the required elements of the content are accurate and complete
- Proofreading — examining material after its textual and visual elements have been laid out to correct any errors and confirm that the design effectively supports communication

As a freelancer, you may be hired to produce or edit any of the writing forms listed above and many others not listed here. In some sectors, certain forms may be more regularly outsourced than others; for instance, the sales-oriented business and technology fields rely heavily on sell sheets, white papers, and case studies. The non-profit world thrives on grants and donations, so their foundation is writing proposals, grant applications, and fundraising letters. You might also choose to write for particular platforms; for example, you could specialize in social media coordination or even focus on a particular platform, like Instagram. Tons of business owners out there are afraid of falling behind on these platforms and are eager for help. Or video script writing for the ready market that is TikTok — again, there's a willing market of senior-level communicators who are terrified of this relatively new platform and looking for a bright (stereotypically young) writer to help them out.

In the editing realm, there are also many places to specialize, including magazine editing, report editing (sometimes in specialized niches like medical or financial reports), book editing, and academic editing. There are also different types of editing, as outlined above, but also different sectors can include specific editing roles. For example, in the book publishing world, a developmental editor helps to assess a manuscript from an initial draft, determines the editing needed, and engages in a structural or substantive edit, ensuring the text has the best structure and readability.

With stylistic editing (also called line editing), copy editing, and proofreading, editors need to become experts on language and usage, focusing on everything from sentence structure to grammar, as well as be proficient at using the common style guides — books outlining established standards for consistency that organizations requiring editing will choose as their baseline. Common style guides such as *The Canadian Press Stylebook*, *The Associated Press Stylebook* (in the United States), and *The Chicago Manual of Style* apply rules to everything from how to format the date (e.g., June 1, 1976, or 1 June 1976) to how to deal with numbers (long-time users of *The Canadian Press Stylebook* will know that you spell out numbers from one to nine and use numerals for 10 and above). An organization may ask its freelancers for one or more types of editing, or it may not know what type of editing the material needs, so you become the expert, look at the manuscript, and educate them. Proofreading is the final stage in editing, where ideally all major issues have been spotted and you are a fresh set of eyes on the text (so don't try to move sentences around unless there's something so outrageous it will cause major embarrassment).

Generalist Versus Specialist?

Another hot topic in freelancing is the decision of whether to offer your services as a generalist or specialist. A generalist is a "will write for money" writer who advertises widely and will take on work from any sector, writing in any form. A specialist targets only one industry (or maybe two) and can offer a narrow range of editorial products, say, a health writer who does website copy or a book editor who edits fiction.

In some ways, the distinction is a bit false. There's not really enough time in the day or year to write about everything, so even generalists end up specializing in a handful of topics, and those are often related. For instance, I consider myself somewhat of a generalist, but most of my topics are in the same work/business realm: technology, careers, business, and my most recent acquisition, education. I would not write about fashion or automotive maintenance, nor would you want me to, as those are not my natural areas of interest.

On the other hand, I have met many specialists who would not turn down a lucrative gig in another niche. They just don't advertise it. And you don't necessarily need to make this decision for eternity. I started out with a much narrower specialization in technology, mostly because it was a topic I liked that happened to be hot at the time I started, in the early 2000s. I gradually expanded into other areas, mostly because I was curious about new topics or opportunities that came along.

If I were writing this chapter ten years ago, I would be recommending both specialist and generalist approaches, but in today's market I would suggest cultivating a specialty, at least to start. A couple of factors prompt this suggestion. First, so many freelancers are starting as specialists, you're competing with writers who already have deeper knowledge of a niche. Also, it gives you a sense of focus for your new business. Of course, don't turn down work outside of your niche, and don't hesitate to add niches or even pivot as the years roll on.

When you're deciding how to specialize, some people choose an industry, say, health care or automotive or financial or gaming or any of the many sectors out there. You can also focus within some industries as a Business-to-Business (B2B) or a Business-to-Consumer (B2C) writer. A good example here is the technology industry, where B2B would be focused on, say, creating materials for a tech company that sells human-resources software to other companies, versus a B2C writer who would create materials to sell to the consumer — for example, writing about the latest smartphone for review websites. Editors also choose sectors to focus on; for example, academic editors edit academic papers, and medical editors may work on medical reports and textbooks as their sole focus.

Other freelancers specialize by content type — for example, grant writing, long-form content, or social media. Still others specialize in both industry and content — for example, writing website copy for dermatologists or blog posts for realtors, where they can showcase their knowledge of the sector alongside the type of writing. The medical editor may transition to editing only textbooks if they can get enough work. Renowned marketer Seth Godin talks about looking for your "smallest viable audience" or the most niched you can get and still have a market of people who want your services. If you get good at writing for this audience, they'll really appreciate that you've tailored your services for their niche and queue up to hire you — in theory. In practice, I'm not sure that you're going to find your forever niche immediately; it will be more of a process of zooming in and out until you find a group that interests you, provides enough work, and sustains your business for the long term.

Also, don't get so hung up on your niche that you hesitate to choose any. In my freelance classes, I sometimes encounter students who refuse to commit to a niche because they don't know what to pick or fear going too small or staying too big. I joke that I'm not going to check up on them in a decade and verify that they're still in the same niche they chose as a first-semester college student.

Seriously, pick a niche, try it out, and if it doesn't seem like you, then pick another.

Figuring Out Your Niche

So, if not your forever niche, then let's pick out your first niche. How do you choose? I think you need to find a marriage between a sector that you're naturally keen on and one that is also lucrative enough to be the basis for a business. I love reading, but, unfortunately, book reviewing gigs are not well paid, not plentiful, and too time-consuming to meet my income goals. I still do book reviewing on the side (and always for pay, even if small), but it's not the major thrust of my business because that niche can't pay the rent.

An ideal niche is one that encompasses many writing avenues: ideally a topic that is covered by magazines and newspapers so writing media articles is an option, but that also encompasses corporate clients requiring marketing materials. Finally, the sector needs to be big enough and rich enough to afford your services.

As a sample sector, consider the health field. Since health is important to every human being, even general newspapers and magazines regularly feature articles on its many aspects. There are also trade or specialty magazines catering to both health professionals (*Canadian Nurse* magazine) and general readers who are interested in health issues (say, readers of *Yoga Journal*).

Even a non-specialist can think of a handful of venues you might write for in health: hospitals, insurance providers, seniors' facilities, fitness businesses, food manufacturers, and more. These corporate clients would also have a need to produce documents regularly: hospitals, for example, require fundraising letters, brochures, annual reports, and marketing materials, just to name a few editorial products. As large, mostly government-funded operations, they would have the money to pay a writer/editor and the interest in impressing donors with editorial materials that are professional and well-written. On the altruistic side of things, it's fun to think that something you write will educate someone about their own health.

The niche that's right for you is often one that you've already shown an interest in. What blogs do you read most? What sections of your newspaper or news websites do you turn to most regularly? What are your hobbies? There may be fields that you already know quite a bit about. Do you have previous experience working or volunteering in a sector?

Choosing an area that matches your natural interests can help you find a topic that's sustainable for you. You may even know enough about the topic to overcome some of the learning curve you'd face to understand the field.

Yet another way to specialize is by type of writing. If you're a social media nut, you might decide that you want to provide only X (formerly Twitter) and Facebook updates to several sectors. There's a writer out there, Gordon Graham, who specializes in writing white papers, a type of corporate essay that helps to explain a technical product in a simplified way (thatwhitepaperguy.com). Indexing (supplying the helpful back matter that aids readers in locating topics within non-fiction texts) is an editing subspecialty — you can connect with some of the Canadian experts in this field through the Indexing Society of Canada (indexers.ca).

You might also consider what types of materials are produced in your niche and whether you like writing those forms. For example, I mentioned that a major focus of the non-profit niche is fundraising, so many of the forms non-profits need are fundraising letters and brochures that focus on telling community stories and related materials.

If you're looking to brainstorm all of the subject matter areas out there, here's a list of a few niches to consider, along with their subsectors:

- Arts (music, dance, art, film, television)
- Education (primary, secondary, post-secondary, private)
- Finance (banking, insurance, brokerages)
- Food and beverage (grocery chains, hotel/restaurant, breweries, wineries)
- Government (federal, provincial, municipal, agencies)
- Health (medical, dental, alternative, pharmaceutical, hospitals)
- Marketing (advertising, public relations)
- Manufacturing/construction (automotive, retail)
- Non-profit (charities, non-governmental organizations)
- Professional services (law, accounting, architecture, engineering)
- Resources (oil and gas, mining)
- Technology (computers, internet, robotics, gaming, web design)
- Trades (plumbing, electrical, contractors)
- Transportation (transit, trucking, aviation)
- Travel and Tourism (travel websites, resorts, airlines)

As you can see, there are many sectors, so it will help to research industries you may not have previously considered. Maybe choose five of your favourites from the above list and search online for publications and businesses that you could write for in that sector. This is called "market research," and it can involve as little as looking online or as much as interviewing potential clients to see if they could use your services. Do they publish a lot of content? Do you like to read it? Would you like to write or edit that content? After looking at a handful, choose the sector that holds your interest and try it out.

For writers or editors who are transitioning to freelance later in their careers, a natural choice can be the niche where you have built your expertise. Likely you'll already have contacts in the industry, and these can become your first clients. If you're going freelance because you hated your career path, is there an adjacent niche that's more palatable? If possible, make life easier for yourself by starting the business in your area of expertise; then, if you want, you can slowly pivot out of it once you are accustomed to running a business. For example, I started in technology but then took on assignments that straddled technology and business before writing straight business stories.

Making Your Idea a Reality

Once you've figured out what niche you'd like to try, think about how exactly to start making your freelance plan a reality. To begin, you'll tackle several starter tasks in tandem, including setting up the basics of your business (business registration, website domain) and developing the basic marketing materials (website, LinkedIn profile). These are covered later on in the business set-up and marketing sections of this book.

Another thing you'll do is start planning your outreach and approaches to clients (see: pitching). As you do so, you'll want to set goals for your business. This is something you should be thinking about from the beginning, which is why I'm focusing on it here.

Goal-Setting

Setting goals for your business is a great way to keep your efforts on track from the beginning. As you achieve each goal, you can take pride in that accomplishment, and if your efforts are moving you more slowly toward your goals than you expected, consider what else you need to do. Sometimes your goals will change, and you'll end up discarding them or setting new ones. But having a plan is helpful.

Initial goals for your business will probably include setting up your operation, finding that first handful of clients, doing marketing and outreach to create and expand your network, and securing a regular client base. There are also some specific types of goals you'll want to consider as you plan your overall business.

FINANCIAL GOALS

I've read that the difference between someone who calls themself a professional and someone who says they're an amateur is that professionals make money at the skill. Do not be content to be in business just for the fun of it — the only way we get to keep doing what we love is to make it pay enough to keep the proverbial roof over our heads and food in our bellies. As you plan out your business, you'll want to take this financial requirement into account and come up with realistic figures for what you can achieve. How much income do you want to make? What is the minimum you could live on as you begin the slow journey of building your business? What is your wildest dream salary and is it possible in your niche of choice? What are the other non-monetary benefits? Yes, yes, occasional Friday afternoon matinees; we've covered that already.

Such decisions may influence the pace at which you start your business. If you need a certain income at all times, you might consider starting your freelance adventure part-time and quitting your steady job only when you are satisfied you can swing it. Warning: you probably won't be able to replace your income in the first year and maybe not in the second. A freelance friend who read this chapter suggested I shouldn't be striking too much optimism into the hearts of readers. So, plan for a possible slow uptake, one that can be affected by outside factors like the economy and the freelance landscape as well as by your efforts. Whether you go the full-time or part-time route to start, try to have that financial-savings cushion to make life easier and give yourself a real chance.

Finding out the going rates in your niche and talking to other freelancers who write in that niche can be excellent ways to gain insight on how much you could earn both at the beginning and with a few years of experience. Search online for salary guides (they aren't great but better than they used to be), join writers' groups, and ask around. Try cold-contacting a writer in your proposed niche and see if they'd be open to a twenty-minute phone call and some direct questions. (I'll share more about pricing in a later chapter.)

Your financial requirements may also influence the types of clients you pursue. Some niches, particularly ones where you're working for organizations whose revenue is based on sales, need copy editing of content or social posts or reports on a regular basis, whether weekly or monthly. Other projects tend to be one-offs, say, an annual report (guess how often that assignment comes along) or a bi-annual magazine. Ideally you want a mix of these projects: steady gigs where the money flows regularly and larger projects that may pay in a big chunk. In choosing a niche, there's a bit of common sense involved in knowing which industries may have richer budgets (hello, financial and legal) and which others may not (hello, crafting? I've been using this niche as a probably unfair example for years, but you do need to be really into it to excel).

Most freelancers also thrive with one or two "anchor clients," steady gigs that tend to provide a regular flow of work and offer stability to your business. For a couple of years early on, I edited a technology magazine called *Information Highways* that published a few times a year and paid my rent so that I didn't have to think afresh about how to make a living every single month. I also did a couple of contracts working for the *Globe and Mail* newspaper on their website relaunches and have taken on stints in agencies as a proofreader for a few weeks. I have since sought out teaching and other longer-term clients to fill this need for ballast and stability. A few years ago, I wrote my first book as a ghostwriter, which filled the same role of a big project that I could carry alongside my regular freelance work. On the flipside, you don't want to have too few clients or rely too heavily on an anchor client, since if you lose them, you will have to replace a big chunk of income quickly. You also want to be careful that you're not working so many hours that you should be considered an employee. I'll discuss these ideas more in later chapters, but it's also something to keep in mind as you plan your financial goals.

THE FORMULA FOR FINANCIAL GOALS
But how do you figure out how to translate your work into your income? You find out how much you need to charge per hour in order to get to your income goal. So, if you want to make $40,000 in your first year, and there are fifty-two weeks in a year, and let's say you take two weeks' vacation to start, that's forty thousand divided by fifty weeks, which equals an income goal of $800 per week. Dividing that weekly income goal by a forty-hour work week means you need to charge $20 per hour. I'll take a moment to shout out to long-time freelancer Paul Lima, whom I've heard repeat this formula many times! His *Six-Figure Freelancer* and other books (found on his website) are gold.

BUT remember that as a self-employed person, you handle all the tasks of the business, including a lot of things you won't get paid for — marketing, IT, researching pitches, and doing client outreach. So, you need to factor in how much time that takes and how many hours are, in fact, billable. Say you decide that you need at least half your week to devote to those unpaid tasks in order to make the other half billable (a reasonable assumption to start). Then your rate is $800 (weekly income goal) divided by twenty hours worked per week, which is $40 per hour. Luckily that's an achievable wage in editorial circles, and once you've been in business a few years you can raise those rates too (please do).

YOUR CREATIVE AND PERSONAL GOALS

While your initial goal may be to get your freelance business off the ground, you may also have creative or personal goals that you want to accomplish with your new writing business. Maybe you want to write at least one investigative magazine article in your first year. Maybe you want to start a successful blog and build a readership.

Maybe you want to strengthen your social media skills so that you can eventually pivot your business in that direction. Maybe you want to write a novel alongside your non-fiction business. Maybe you want to land a feature in a major national magazine or, for Canadians, your first major national AMERICAN magazine (we dream about your higher dollar, U.S. friends). These creative and personal goals should also factor into your planning, since achieving them will give you great satisfaction and may be central to why you started on your freelance journey in the first place.

Although this book is focused mostly on your professional life, your actual life contains more than work, and part of planning out your freelancing life is accounting for how the rest of your life fits around it. I've always liked travelling, so one big attraction for me was that freelancing offered a flexible enough schedule that I could plan longer trips. Freelancers with children value that their flexible schedule allows them to walk their kids to school every day. Some writers like to work late over several weekdays to create long weekends off. Whatever you plan for your personal life, think about how it fits with your freelancing and how those goals might affect your business planning. You may decide to work fewer hours based on the goal of spending time with your young kids and leave the higher wage until later. Or you may decide to find a niche that pays higher so you can work fewer hours.

Your Benefits

While you're thinking about your financial life, another factor that falls into that category is how to take care of yourself when you need medical attention. As a freelancer, nobody pays for your sick days, and there's no fund to access when you need the extra support that comes from employee benefits, such as coverage of your prescription eyewear, your dental visits (that's my specialty), or your prescriptions. To clarify, there's no fund unless you set one up. Fortunately, for Canadians, we have a socialized health care system to rely on, but there's a lot not covered under that, so you need to decide whether it's worth applying for private benefits.

Here is another occasion when it's helpful to ask around the freelance community and learn about the options out there. When I was doing this research for myself, I called a couple of corporate benefits providers and also looked into the plan I finally took up, the Writers' Coalition plan. Offered in Canada to writers and editors via several of the professional editorial associations, it piggybacks on the health plan provided to members of the Alliance of Canadian Cinema, Television and Radio Artists (ACTRA). With thirty thousand members representing multiple times more workers than all of the Canadian writers' associations combined, I find the Writers' Coalition (ACTRA) benefits package to be the best rate for the benefits. Because the amount that I pay in prescriptions (and that damned dental!) is more than I would spend on the monthly premiums, it seems worth it to me (plus the peace of mind from the accident benefits and travel insurance). When I did my informal survey of the freelance community, nearly 37 percent of people said they don't have a benefits plan, 10 percent were part-time freelancers with benefits through their day jobs, almost 22 percent had private benefits, and almost 32 percent had benefits through their spouses.

Your Retirement

Along the lines of benefits, another practical adult topic is retirement. Yes, it will probably come sooner than we expect, and yes, another downside of freelancing is that it doesn't come with a pension plan (but think of the upsides!). In my survey of other Canadian freelancers, approximately 11 percent said they had no retirement savings; at the other end of the spectrum, 13 percent put over a quarter of their income into savings. Between those camps, 22 percent put away less than 5 percent of their income, almost 40 percent said that 15 percent of their income went to savings, and almost 15 percent said they saved 15 to 25 percent of their income for their retirement.

When asked to identify all the savings vehicles they used, 81 percent of the freelancers surveyed noted their savings were in Registered Retirement Savings Plans (RRSPs), over 74 percent specified Tax Free Savings Accounts (TFSAs), with other registered savings accounts, regular savings accounts, and a spouse's pension among the other top choices. I personally set aside 10 percent of my income for RRSPs and TFSAs, although the survey responses are prompting me to think I should increase my own savings ☺.

As a long-time self-employed person, I regret to report a bit of a bias by the banks or perhaps just a failure to notice that my income works differently from incomes in traditional jobs. I love the idea of regular withdrawals to automate my savings, but I often get paid in lump-sum cheques for larger projects, so sometimes my bank account looks pretty low, even though a windfall is imminent. When the Big Cheque lands, this is when I try to pay money into my savings. I also maintain an emergency fund and have a line of credit that I use when I'm paid late (grab those line of credit offers with both hands when they're offered, although do keep tabs on your borrowing). I was especially impressed with long-time freelance copywriter Steve Slaunwhite, who shared that he gives himself a paycheque every two weeks, with regular raises over the years. Another way to automate payment is to transfer what is manageable into a separate account.

Despite the banks not quite understanding my style of work, they are still ready and willing to set us freelancers up with a retirement strategy. I recommend doing that as soon as you can and figuring out a plan for how to get started regardless of how long you're in this lifestyle. If you go back to a traditional job, do take all the benefits that offers, but just because you're self-employed, there's no reason not to think about your future and plan for retirement and all of the adulting that we dread but do because we know it's good for us. A final note: when I posted my question about saving for retirement to an international writer listserv that I belong to (to expand the perspective from my Canadian survey), it initiated a small storm of responses, including admissions of shame from writers who said they didn't have retirement plans and a spectrum of answers that ranged from lump-sum savings to automated solutions. Many lamented that they wished they had thought about retirement planning earlier, and others said that they appreciated the chance to discuss a taboo topic. But as the saying goes, the best time to plant a tree was twenty years ago, and the second-best time is today, so it's a case of moving as soon as you can to put that plan in place.

Your Business Plan

When I created my business, I did so with the help of a business coach who encouraged me to start with market research to figure out what clients and editors in my niche were looking for, then to write a business plan that laid out simple goals for the year, and to schedule monthly tasks to make the goals happen.

Typical business plans for a writer might describe your business and goals, including your niche and the clients you will serve. Write a focused description of the possible markets within your niche (for healthcare, you might talk about healthcare publications plus the health-related businesses in your area that could be potential clients) and current trends within your niche. (Is there a high demand for content? What forms? If fashion, maybe there's a lot of video content created currently.) If you want to edit books, research the independent presses and analyze the number and types of books they publish annually. Another section of the plan can capture your research on pricing within your niche (shows you have a sense of the income potential). Divide your action plan into a handful of initial steps, then set goals you'd like to achieve in a year. In short, the plan should show your understanding of the business you want to create and how you plan to tackle it — the kind of thing you could show to a banker to get a response that sounds like, "This person has clearly done some research, has a realistic grasp of this industry, and a solid idea — I think I will fund this person generously" (haha, probably not that last part).

Today, I take a less formal approach, making time every year to reflect on what goals I will set for the next year. I also think about what worked and what didn't in the past year. For example, one year I wrote a weekly blog for both my author website, suzannebowness.com, and my business website, codeword.ca, and found that for the immense time it took, I wasn't seeing much return. I decided instead to cut the author blog, and I pivoted to sharing the business posts both on the business site and on LinkedIn for a better return on my time investment.

I set annual income targets, generally aim to test out a couple of new markets, and set creative writing goals. A few years ago, for example, I decided to experiment with boosting my X (formerly Twitter) presence, to get back into book reviewing, to expand my reading of international media (to find more story ideas), and to try breaking into at least a couple of American magazines. I also vowed to finish my second poetry collection and send it out to publishers, where it is currently enduring rejection. But at least it's out there. This year my goals are to post weekly on LinkedIn, my new visibility platform of choice; to explore two new niches; and to find more regular anchor clients or retainers to add even more stability to my business. I usually base my income goals on what I made the year before and on how I can go after higher-paid projects in order to make more time for new projects. If I think of an income goal annually, say, $100,000, and break it down by month, say, $8,000 ($100,000 divided by twelve), then I think of the kinds of projects I need to land to make that up, say, one website writing project ($3,000), an annual report ($4,000), and a couple of blog posts ($500 times two). Personal goals might include taking a month off to travel in the summer.

While I do my grand check-in and planning at the beginning of the year, I also verify monthly to see how on track I am, especially with my financial goals. If I'm really off-track, I brainstorm ways that I can get back on. Could I send some more pitches? Have I been attending too many afternoon matinees and need to trade those for some late nights at my desk? Is the new niche I explored not as lucrative as I thought? Keeping a regular eye on my habits and my goals helps to make sure I steer my little business ship to safety before it floats too far off course.

Exercises

EXERCISE 1
Look at the list of niches in this chapter. Which ones naturally interest you? Are there any where you have previous experience? Are there any niches that you've never considered? Narrow your choices down to between three and five, including one that you've never thought about, and do some internet research to find out more about that industry. Can you figure out what writing forms might be standard in that sector? What publications are available to write for? What are the subsectors within that sector (e.g., yoga studios and physiotherapists in the wellness space)? Based on your research, does one sector appeal more than it did before?

EXERCISE 2
What are some of your business goals? Brainstorm a list of possible goals for your first year in business. Then brainstorm your upcoming personal, creative, lifestyle, and financial goals, and think about how they will fit with your business.

Chapter 3

Just the Business Basics, Baby

If you start telling people that you are in business and you get an assignment tomorrow, start working on that assignment. Setting up your business is important, but perhaps the most fundamental piece of it is declaring yourself in business (I am writer!) and getting to work. One strong upside of a writing or editing business is that it doesn't require any special licencing or any tools beyond a computer. Okay, the internet is quite helpful too. Anyway, here are the technical requirements for running a business.

Just a reminder that I'm based in Canada, so I'm going to reference this country (and even my home province of Ontario) while also talking generally about other countries. Be sure to look up the rules in your area. I should also repeat my mantra that I am neither a financial nor a legal professional, and any notes I make below should be double-confirmed for your business.

First step: name your business. Many writers will operate under their own names, and so my business name might be Suzanne Bowness. You can also choose a fun name, especially if you think you might grow beyond one person, as I did with CodeWord when I created my business. At the time, I was doing both writing and web design and thought myself clever: Code+Word — you're nodding in approval, aren't you? Until I dropped the web part of my business, and now I field questions about whether, in fact, CodeWord is some sort of spy agency or hacker outfit or phishing operation.

Actually, even when I settled on my clever, now-not-so-clever name, I was on the fence about it. Again, it's one of these elements you could overthink forever, so just choose something and get on with it, since nothing should delay you getting to that sweet, sweet business-building.

Business Name Registration

Once you've named your business, you have the option to register it and get a business number. If you are operating under your own name, as many writers and editors do, it's not required until you need to charge GST/HST, at which point you'll get one when you register to collect this tax. If you choose a fancy name like CodeWord, you do need to register your business. If you call yourself Suzanne Bowness Consulting or Suzanne Bowness & Associates, you need to register it. Anything beyond your own name (this applies for most jurisdictions).

In Canada, business registrations are handled at the provincial or territorial levels. There are also different types of businesses you can register, depending on the work and complexity of structure. Many writing businesses start out as sole proprietorships, meaning that the owner and the business are one entity. Other types of business registry include incorporation or other formats that create a new legal entity for the business (whereby you would take a salary from the business as its owner/employee). If there will be two people owning the business, you may want to register a partnership.

Where I live, in Ontario, registering your business name gets you a Master Business Licence, which currently costs $60 for five years. You can do this online. You need to search your business name to make sure it is unique. If CodeWord had been taken, I might have had to call it CodeWord Communications (which I do, as my operating name). If you want to change the structure of your business, you may have to register for a new business number. Registering a small business differs by province and state, and even by municipality, so be sure to ask around your freelancer community when you set up and look into your municipal and provincial government small-business resources to see if there are any self-employment regulations you should be aware of. Some provinces include a federal business number as part of your provincial registration, while others do not. You may need to register your business even if you are not registering a business name, and you will need to include self-employment income on your taxes.

In the United States, you similarly do not need to register your business if you are operating under your own legal name. However, there may be tax-related and other benefits for registering. Business registration options are similar: sole proprietorship, partnership, and corporation, plus LLC (limited liability company), which is a hybrid of corporation and partnership (and where you do need to register a business name). As a sole proprietor, you can pay tax using your social security number as your taxpayer identification number or, in some cases, apply for an employer identification number (EIN) from the American Internal Revenue Service (IRS) if you have employees or for other reasons (like GST/HST registration, the EIN helps signal that you're an independent contractor, so that may be attractive for professionalism reasons). Americans pay self-employment tax (a percentage that includes Social Security and Medicare taxes) on earnings of $400 or more, in addition to income tax. Each state has different licensing rules for different business types, so again, get to know your freelance community and ask around.

In the United Kingdom, freelancers or "sole traders" don't need to officially register a business name, but you will want to register as self-employed with HM Revenue and Customs. You only need to charge the Value Added Tax (VAT) if you earn over a certain threshold, currently ninety thousand pounds, although you can voluntarily register before that. Again, check your local area regarding other registrations.

If you do register your business name in Ontario, registration will need to be renewed in five years (check the expiry time frame in your area); immediately add the reminder to renew to your calendar. Apparently, nobody comes and carts you away if you don't, but it is a panic-inducing thing to lose that registration. Speaking on behalf of a friend, of course.

Procedures for any other business types are a little more involved but could be beneficial depending on the business. You should consult with your accountant and see what works for you. When I asked my long-standing accountant a few years ago if I should finally upgrade to incorporation, she asked if I had employees (no, outside of my part-time virtual assistant, whom I pay through an agency) and suggested that if I was still solo then the tax and cost hassle was probably not worth it (you have to do taxes for both yourself and the corporation once you've registered — it really is like creating a new person). Others feel strongly about the benefit of separating yourself so that anyone suing your business would not be able to access assets you personally own, such as your house. I've heard that incorporation is highly recommended in more complex industries like film, where a larger crew and more moving parts leave you at higher litigation risk. So far, I'm still a sole proprietor.

Definitely get a lawyer to look over the paperwork if you do any registrations for a more complex business structure like incorporation; it may cost a little more (I've heard in the few hundred to thousands of dollars range when you factor in fees and legal advice), but the peace of mind would be worth it.

Domain Names and Social Media Handles

Other essentials you'll want to set up early include registering a domain name for your website, claiming your LinkedIn page (both your name and your business name) if you don't have one, and claiming handles on any social media accounts.

Ideally your social media accounts and websites should be consistent with each other; for example, my business name is CodeWord Communications, and my Instagram and Facebook handles are @codeword or some variation. If you already have a personal account on X (formerly Twitter), consider whether to set up a new account for your professional life or to continue with your current account (perhaps just add fewer cat-related posts if the latter). Many people also use their names on X; this is what I do. I did use @codeword for years and decided to switch over to my name, but in the few seconds when I grabbed @suzannebowness, somebody else snapped up @codeword before I could lock it down again. Do as I say, people, not as I do. Even if you're not planning to use the handles immediately, try registering your name on all platforms just so you have them in future. You never know when a Twitter is going to go into decline or a TikTok is going to blow up, and you'll want to be prepared by having claimed new spaces if needed. I'd also set up a dedicated work email account that looks professional: firstname.lastname@gmail.com (when your website is ready, you can switch over to writer@businessname.com). When new platforms come out (hello, Mastodon and Threads), you should probably check them out and register a name just in case.

Domain names, as you know from being an internet user, come with several extensions, the most popular being .com, .net, .ca (in Canada), and .org. You register the domain names via a registrar or hosting company, which also has search functions so you can see if your name or business name is available in the various extensions. A domain name registration costs around $10 to $20 per year, and you can register for several years at once. Even if you are doing business under a business name, it makes sense to register at least yourname.com if it is available, just so you have it and nobody else can post there.

Where possible, try to register your .com domain name, as .com is the most popular extension. You should also consider registering other extensions, both because you can forward them to your main domain and because registering domains prevents others from registering them. If you have a popular name, like John Smith, and the domain is taken, consider how else you could word your domain — for example, johnsmithwriter.com. I have registered suzannebowness.com, suebowness.com (which I point to suzannebowness.com), codeword.ca (codeword.com was not available, so I decided not to be a crybaby about it and registered my next best option), and of course, feistyfreelancer.com.

It's important to keep your domain name renewal in your calendar, since if it expires, there are predatory individuals who thrive on snapping them up. These thieves will even try to extort you, threatening to redirect the domain name to porn sites if you don't pay hundreds of dollars. As someone who used to design websites for other writers, I have been through this very catastrophe with a writer client.

Once you have your domain, build your site on one of many platforms. Thankfully, creating websites is easier for the non-technical human than it ever has been. Check out the WordPress platform (WordPress.com is a free hosted platform that includes ads whereas WordPess.org is included with most web hosts). Wix, Weebly, and Squarespace are other popular platforms. Each offers a wide variety of customizable templates. There are also many plug-ins to monitor and enhance your site and to track statistics as well as YouTube videos to help get you started, and web designers to help you tweak your website even further.

While you can upload a site for free and point your domain name to it, eventually you may want to also sign up for some space with a hosting company, which skips the ads that free services often require and costs as little as $10 to $15 per month (and up to $30 to $50) for all the space you would need. Some packages also offer free domain registration with a hosting account. It's worth spending an afternoon exploring and figuring out which package is right for you.

I should also mention I'm aware that the writer website has passed its heyday, and I do know some successful freelancers who operate with just their LinkedIn page as a place for their portfolio pieces. Even my informal writer survey said so; while 38 percent had both a website and LinkedIn page, 32 percent had only a LinkedIn page but no website. But I'll never give my website up — a place where I can exert control over what comes up when you google my name, plus it allows me to choose my best samples and present my writer/editor/consultant brand the way I want to express it, all tidy in a link that I can send to new prospects. Not that I'm against the LinkedIn profile; in fact, I recommend new writers create that first and leave the website as a medium-term first-year project.

Oh, and as long as you are creating a website, why not create some business cards too? They're great for networking events and as a place to list your website address, along with your email address, LinkedIn profile address, and phone number. Also add your new contact details to your email signature. Might as well advertise everywhere that's easy — you're in business!

Collecting Tax

Once you have set up your business registration and you have your business number, you need to register to collect whatever taxes are applicable in your area. In Canada, that's the Goods and Services Tax (GST) or, in some provinces, the Harmonized Sales Tax (HST), which represents a blend of provincial sales tax and GST.

Actually, you're not technically required to charge GST/HST until you are making over $30,000 per year, but as someone pointed out to me early on, if you are a full-time freelancer and don't charge GST/HST, you are sending a signal that you don't make more than that sum, whereas you'd probably like to create the image that you are rich and successful from the start. I have met many part-time freelancers that do not collect GST/HST, so it's a personal call ($30,000 would be a pretty healthy side hustle if you had a full-time job). One of the most helpful pieces of advice my accountant passed along is that you must start collecting GST/HST *not by calendar year* but as soon as you hit the $30,000 mark. If that happens in September, that's when you need to collect GST/HST, and if you think the Canada Revenue Agency is not going to take note, you would be wrong. Once you do start collecting GST/HST, you have to include your GST/HST number on every invoice and submit that money to the government annually (or quarterly if you make over a certain amount).

As an example, in the province of Ontario, where I reside, the GST/HST rate is currently set at 13 percent. The choice of the word "collect" is deliberate here. While you get to charge an extra 13 percent, you are holding it for the government; you should keep it in a separate bank account so you can hand it over come tax time.

To register for GST/HST, you contact the Canada Revenue Agency, and they assign you a GST/HST number. You then paste the number at the bottom of your invoices and add the GST amount to be collected to your bottom line. You must collect this tax based on the province where your client resides. For my client in the province of Saskatchewan, where the tax rate is only 5 percent, for example, my invoice is $1,000 plus 5 percent, for a total of $1,050. For my client in the province of Nova Scotia, where the tax rate is 15 percent, my invoice is $1,000 plus $150, for a total of $1,150. Then I put the $150 in a special bank account I've created for GST/HST collection, and the rest of the payment is deposited in my regular account. Again, finance people notice. Miffed accounting department types have definitely called to correct me when I forget and include my home province tax on their invoice instead of theirs, and I've felt the shame of having to correct and resubmit my invoices more than once.

For Canadians doing business in the U.S., you don't charge any tax but, instead, download and fill in a W8-BEN form that establishes with the IRS that you are a non-U.S. taxpayer who has received U.S. income (this is based on an intergovernmental agreement between Canada and the U.S.). Send in the form along with your invoice and share the income amount with your accountant at tax time. You need to update the W8-BEN form every three years, and you can search online to find the form.

While we're on the topic of registering for things (an awkward segue, but I can't figure out where else to put this essential information), Canadians should also be aware of Access Copyright, a collective that allocates compensation to writers for their work that is used (photocopied, etc.) by educational institutions, businesses, governments, and others. You need to sign up for the program, then update your account with a list of published work you produce each year. The fund is allocated equally to all writers plus extra for your specific work. A similar program for books, called the Public Lending Right, sends yearly payments to creators whose works are in Canada's public libraries (to quote their website). Check into both of these once you've been in business for a few months to make sure you're getting the money you're owed!

Taxes in General

Collecting tax is about as far as I go solo in this important financial domain. As a self-employed person, your taxes are going to be more complex than the traditional worker's taxes. You're already putting your tax money in a special bank account so you can pay the government at the end of the year. If your tax bill is higher than $3,000, in Canada you will be required to pay that tax in quarterly installments throughout the year, and you're charged interest if you don't remit. Canada Revenue Agency can also ask you to pay your HST/GST quarterly.

Because employers take deductions from employee paycheques, and you no longer have an employer, you'll have to make all the contributions to Canada Pension Plan (CPP) via your annual tax filing; self-employed people pay both the employer's contribution and the employee's contribution, so basically paying twice. You can also choose to pay into Employment Insurance, which can be helpful, for example, if you're planning to take a parental leave, but you have to carefully weigh the amount you're paying in with what you would receive. I have always found it works better for me to keep an emergency fund for slow times.

Something fun on the tax side is that you can reduce your tax bill by deducting some of the expenses that you pay to run a business. These are the infamous "write-offs" that you may have heard about.

Yes, it's true, you can write off everything from restaurant bills (provided you took a client out to lunch) to networking events (provided you met with colleagues and talked business) to your work tools (laptops, cellphones, even magazine subscriptions) to professional memberships and conferences. You can even write off a percentage of your rent or a percentage of the interest on your mortgage (interest on the mortgage, not on the principal) provided that you have a dedicated office space to work on your business (yes, a tiny corner of your living room counts, but you have to work there over 50 percent of the time and use the space only to earn employment income). I write off all of the above, including the percentage of square feet (and utilities, including electricity, heat) that I use for my home office. Self-employed people can also write off a percentage of their property taxes and home insurance.

Keep records of these business-building activities every year by holding onto receipts. Write a note for yourself on the back of the receipts to indicate what they were for, then turn the shoebox-full over to your accountant at tax time so they can use the receipts to reduce your tax bill. Or rather, the deductions reduce the amount of income and, therefore, tax you owe on it. There are also fancy apps that take a photo of your receipt and add it to your filing. Keep in mind that these write-offs are usually only percentages; for example, 50 percent of restaurant meal expenses qualify (so only take your editor out for a really fancy meal if you genuinely like them, not because you think the write-off will be higher). You can write off long-distance calls and a portion of your phone that you use for business (or all of a dedicated business line). You can deduct salaries you pay to other people (in my case, to my virtual assistant); office expenses; advertising and promotion, such as business cards; and also courses you take to upgrade your skills. Your work tools are deducted on a depreciating basis (so a percentage of your laptop is written off in the first year and lower percentages in subsequent years). If you're still keeping paper receipts, know that cash register tape can fade, so you should be making copies of those receipts (taking a photo with your phone works well), as the CRA can ask to review up to the past seven years of taxes (or they can decide to audit you). It may be worth investing in that bookkeeping app after all.

Your Accountant

All this tax talk calls to mind one of the most important people in your new business life: your accountant. Not only can they help you navigate the more complex tax rules of the self-employed, but they know more about deductions, and they save you time. They'll even show you the quick method of calculating your GST/HST owed, which allows you to keep a fraction of the percentage for collecting it (ask your accountant about the quick method if they don't mention it).

I didn't need convincing on this topic, but if you need an argument to hire someone, consider how much time it would take you to do your own complex taxes versus someone who actually knows what they're doing. And they'll do a better job. And you can write off their fee. If you want to maximize the value of your accountant's time, you'd be wise to present your accountant with a tidy spreadsheet of your incoming earnings and your outgoing expenses (or the output of that app you invested in) rather than your shoebox of receipts. Just list all your incoming money (invoices to clients) and outgoing expenses (receipts) by month. You may also want to list by tax-friendly categories, such as entertainment, travel, and professional memberships. I keep track of mine in simple Excel spreadsheets, although I am in the midst of joining the twenty-first century and moving to a bookkeeping program.

Keeping good records also has the benefit of letting you see where you spend your money (okay, I'm just trying to find a positive spin on this topic — I really think of record-keeping as a huge drag but a necessary evil). Possibly the best news in this vein is that in Canada you actually get an extra six weeks to file your tax return — yes, the deadline for freelancers to file their tax returns is June 15. And your partner gets the extension too — when my accountant, Sunny, guest speaks in my writing classes, she always jokes that the self-employed could use that as a pickup line.

To find the right accountant, ask other writers for referrals. Ideally hire someone who specializes in working with the self-employed. You can even find those whose niche is specifically arts professionals and who will be the most familiar with our specific deductions. Never be afraid to ask for references or to fire an accountant who does not respect your business. Big shout-out here to my accountant, Sunny Widerman, of Personal Tax Advisors, who met all of the above criteria and is responsible for most pro tips I've sprinkled through this text. One reason I appreciate Sunny's willingness to explain tax stuff to an artsy like me is because I once hired her opposite — an accountant who remarked on how small my income was in my first year, after I'd spent months working my tail off. That was when I realized you can fire someone who treats you badly — joke's on you, sir.

Tools and Technology

As I mentioned earlier, a big bonus of the writing business is the low barrier to entry. No freelancer application form. Not even expensive upfront costs. Unlike graphic designers, you don't need expensive software programs but, rather, just your good old laptop, which you likely own or have access to already. Add in the internet and a smartphone and you're golden. A printer is handy, though less necessary; I used to list fax machine and scanner for returning signed contracts, although most publications now send contracts via email, and younger people are even starting to look puzzled when I mention a fax machine. A few smaller publications will ask you to take a photo if you're covering an event, but most use professional photographers, and cellphone cameras have improved to the point where they work in a pinch.

I recently gave up my land line after many years of hanging onto it, now that the cell networks are reliable enough to have fewer dropped calls than in the past. A phone headset or earpiece can be invaluable, freeing up your hands to type notes as you do telephone interviews. You'll want an application to record your interviews, whether it be a digital recorder or an app that you can download on your smartphone. If you still have a landline, there's a handy cord that you can plug into the end of your phone and into your recorder to record calls. Feel free to describe it that way when you stop by the electronics store.

Creative types have a penchant for Apple, but a PC is fine too. In terms of software, Microsoft Word with its Track Changes function for editing is useful and pretty universally used, although in the past five years, Google Docs has started to take over because their changes tool is (almost, not really, not quite) equally functional and their programs are free. You may also need to access some spreadsheet programs (MS Excel or Google Sheets), and if you work for a small publication and offer services beyond writing, you could be asked to use programs like Adobe InDesign (a standard layout program) or Photoshop (a photo editing program). Other digital firms, like Canva, offer graphic design tools so easy that even a writer can learn them. You should get familiar with some file-sharing programs (Google Drive is popular, as is DropBox), project management platforms (Trello, Asana, Basecamp), chat programs (Slack is popular with office types at the moment), and a calendar app/scheduler if you do a lot of interviews.

I have an external hard drive to back up my work. As an aside, I strongly recommend backing up your work, since losing your writing means losing time and money — my external hard drive pulls my work off my computer every hour. There are also online services that you can use. Protecting your computer with anti-virus software can also help to stave off viruses that can slow or shut down your system, another productivity killer.

I pay for a few tech tools, like a video conferencing subscription (current favourites include Zoom and Skype), a newsletter platform, and a social media scheduler. I try other tools periodically to see if they work for me and whether the cost is worth the time savings. Editorial support tools like PerfectIt are also helpful to improve consistency as an editor. In five years, feel free to <insert here> whatever artificial intelligence (AI) tool has emerged as most useful.

Books and Reference Tools

Other tools for writers include a good dictionary (even in this digital age), a grammar resource (for settling arguments), and relevant style guides. *The Canadian Press Stylebook*, with its smaller companion, *Caps and Spelling*, is used in Canada by news publications and corporations. *The Chicago Manual of Style* is used by most magazines and book publishers. *The MLA Style Manual and Guide to Scholarly Publishing* and the *Publication Manual of the American Psychological Association* are used as reference systems in the academic arts and sciences fields, respectively. In the United States, *The Associated Press Stylebook* is the equivalent of *The Canadian Press Stylebook* (probably the first time a sentence has referenced the little country's book as the standard to compare to the equivalent in the populous country).

Good books about writing are nice to have around for inspiration: see my list in Appendix A, but Stephen King's *On Writing*, William Zinsser's *On Writing Well*, and Anne Lamott's *Bird by Bird* are three popular books that I like. Editors Canada publishes a set of Professional Editorial Standards. *Elements of Indigenous Style* by Gregory Younging has become a go-to resource for editors and publishers.

Does a good desk chair need to be mentioned? Probably, as you'll be spending a lot of time there. A designated workspace is ideal. Good lighting, both general and task. A window is nice if you can get one. Having two monitors so that I can spread out my digital windows has been life changing!

Insurance and Other Protection

Finally, it's not technically a tool but it is equally essential — think about how you'll cover the elements that an employer often provides. In my discussion on financial goal-setting, I looked at some options for health insurance, either through private benefits or a spouse. Spend some time asking fellow freelancers about their decisions and weighing your options.

Another kind of insurance that writers can get is called professional liability (sometimes called errors and omissions) insurance, which covers the writer if you make a mistake on a project and the client sues you. Say you wrote an advertisement for a product, and you wrote that the price was $100 when it was really $1,000. The client could argue they lost revenue due to your error in leaving off the zero. In my unscientific freelancer survey, only 16 percent of respondents reported having professional liability insurance. One reason many writers do not have errors and omissions insurance is that it's expensive, though it is increasingly being required by some clients, particularly in government. For most writers, the best approach is to educate yourself about price points and consider getting the insurance if a client comes along who demands it. This happened to me a few years ago with both a university and a government client, so I'm now covered for about $2 million (a standard request at this point) by a policy that includes a deductible. Initially I found an insurer through a broker, but when I discovered that one of the professional associations I belong to also offers it through a group plan, I switched.

Are you in business yet? You will be after you've moved through this to-do list. Actually, the list is not really that long, so I'd keep reading to the pitching chapters so you can start your client outreach at the same time as you are setting these pieces up. Certainly, do not wait until your website is perfect and your business cards are printed, as I've seen other writers do, letting weeks go by. Instead, make day one the day you send your first pitch and create your LinkedIn page, starting both the creative and administrative side of your business at the same time.

Exercises

EXERCISE 1
Make a list of things you currently have for your business and things that you may need to acquire. Where would you conduct your business? Think about the office or desk space that you have and how you could set it up to be more permanent and suited to your editorial business.

EXERCISE 2
Consider the registrations that you need to set up for your business. How do you envision operating as a business owner? Have you thought of a name for your business? (Is the domain name available?) What are the registration requirements for establishing a business in your area? Make yourself a checklist of start-up tasks.

Chapter 4

Reading Like a Writer

By now you are itching to begin freelancing, to start pitching and creating. But before we move on to the pitching chapter, let's return to your roots as a reader. For me and for many of my colleagues and students, reading was the way we came to writing. I was a big fiction reader in childhood and as a teenager (and still am), then started reading magazines and appreciating their non-fiction storytelling as well. I tell my students that the best way to become a better writer is to read widely — subscribe to magazines, read online, read non-fiction books, and keep up that fiction habit if you have one. In other words, never lose the love of reading that brought you here in the first place. I would say the same for editors, that continued reading helps with understanding the way sentences are constructed and absorbing new approaches to structure, all of which can only help with your career. But now also add another layer as a reader — reading like a writer. For my second-career free-lancers, you already know this, but maybe it's been a while since you've read with the notion of pitching at the back of your mind, so hopefully this advice will reconnect you with that early excitement or even help you to ponder a new niche. Editors, this chapter is less focused on you, but it can be if it inspires you to take up a sideline in writing like I have with editing. At minimum it will help you better understand the writer's thought process as we're coming up with the texts that you help us to polish.

When you pick up a magazine and notice you're enjoying a feature or profile, read it a second time and try to understand some of the reasons why. Does the writer open with a scene that makes you laugh out loud? Is there nice imagery and turns of phrase sprinkled throughout? Does the article make you think about something familiar in a new way? All of these are great writing techniques that you can bring into your own writing. With a story you really enjoy, you can even go as far as to create a "reverse outline" — an exercise I do with my students — where you look at the story and recreate the outline you imagine the writer could have made to come up with the article. It's a great learning tool.

But before the writing comes the idea. As a reader-turned-writer, your job is not just to appreciate a good idea but also to become an idea hunter, a mercenary for the next angle that you can pitch. Let's think about how to do that hunting first.

Finding a Good Story Idea

While great story ideas may be hard to come by, you'll know them when you hear them. And there's nothing like a great idea to level the playing field for those starting out. A new writer with a stellar idea that only they can write will vault over those of us with decades of experience and get the assignment. Ideas are the holy grail that will get you published, at least in journalism, which for many nonfiction writers is an ideal starting point.

And you know a great idea when you hear it. Think back to the last time you heard of an app or invention that seemed at once novel and yet naturally filled a need. Uber, for example, while a disruption to the taxi industry, just strikes you as a solution to a problem that nobody had yet articulated — those who have cars and a bit of time on their hands offer a lift to those who have a need to get somewhere and have a bit of money on their hands. Perfect story. Almost.

Another element you need for a good story pitch is someone in mind to star in the story. Readers (and editors) are not nearly as interested in ideas as they are in people. So that means if they find Uber intriguing, they'll be even more fascinated by the story of the college student who was able to pay off his student loans by becoming an Uber driver. Or the elderly woman who couldn't afford to get to her medical appointments until her daughter connected her with a driver who now takes her everywhere. You need to find not only the idea but also people (or "characters" — yes, non-fiction borrows the language of fiction all the time) who make you care about the idea.

Other elements you're looking for in a story idea are drama, conflict, and narrative. So, in the Uber case, the drama is in the fact that the service totally disrupts a major industry. Again, how is that story about a person? It's the story of the cabbie who has been driving for twenty-five years and has just had half of his income taken away by the service. Editors buy ideas, but even more so, they buy concrete narratives.

Finally, I'm sorry to ruin this story for you, but the fact that I can use Uber as an example and trust that a reader is familiar enough with the app to know what I'm talking about means it's probably too late to do a first story on that company. If you were going to do a story on Uber today, you'd need to find a new angle on it: like a woman who felt shut out of the male-dominated taxi industry and used Uber to realize her dream of driving for a living, or a lesser-known business that's a spin-off of Uber. Nowadays the Uber example is so well-known that new start-ups are sometimes defined as "the Uber of <insert industry>"; for example, a business called Pawshake that matches pet owners with affordable dog walkers and cat sitters is easily summarized as "Uber for pets." So, a story on the Pawshake start-up could be a new angle (my caveat here is that I learned about this business about five years ago on the nightly news, so it's been covered at least once by a major media outlet and is too far into operation to be seen as new — although if Pawshake newly opens in your small town, feel free to borrow the idea for your local newspaper).

Sometimes new freelancers worry their ideas will be stolen by an unscrupulous editor. I'm not saying this travesty never happens, but ideas are often in the public chatter, the zeitgeist, so you may think they're original but others are aware. If you come up with an idea around the holidays, you can bet a lot of people are thinking about jingle bells and toboggan rides too. Also, most ideas are a dime a dozen — that's why you can't copyright an idea; you can only copyright the actual creation. On occasion, you will pitch a story and the publication truly is working on the story already. Or they may have a writer that takes on those ideas. I once pitched a publication that liked my idea but preferred their in-house writer. So, they bought my idea: an easy hundred dollars.

Omigod (you're thinking). So how do I find ideas before they even get into the news? That's a good question, and a big challenge. Some of my approaches include the following:

- talking to everyone I know about the fact that I'm looking for great ideas and inviting their input
- paying attention at parties and eavesdropping on public transit
- reading widely, including in international media to see if there are any ideas that I can translate to Canada or in local media to see if there's a story to pitch nationally

- reading specialized magazines to see if there are trends and ideas that I could pitch to general magazines (and vice versa)
- connecting with PR professionals in my niche to find out about new trends

Another avenue, and this approach can be a real advantage for a new writer, is to find a story with which you have a personal connection. I recently wrote a story about my adopted mother's reconnection in her sixties with her birth family. Not only was it a neat (strange) opportunity to meet my relatives for the first time via phone interview, but it was a story that I had a unique vantage on and ended up selling to a national magazine (*Zoomer*!). I've had students write about their sibling's medical condition, their own medical condition, their hobby of playing with Lego as an adult, and operations on their family dairy farm — all stories that only they could write, and I was so impressed with them for going for it.

While stories like this don't fall into your lap every day, you should mine any personal connections you may have — maybe you just happen to have gone to high school with an Olympian, or you're taking classes at a yoga studio with a new type of yoga (spynga, anyone? Google it), or you have a pet with a rare disease. All of these are fodder for stories that you would have a new angle on, and these can be the best way to get your first assignment if you don't have a lot of experience as a writer. Another pro tip: keep a notebook and/or notes file on your phone for your ideas so you don't forget them.

And now that you're a pro at ideas, let's turn our writerly eye to publications so we can decode them and make an informed approach.

Pitching Publications

Besides a phenomenal story idea, another must-have for a successful pitch to a magazine, newspaper, website, or other media outlet is a good understanding about the kinds of stories they already publish. Read back quite far into the publication's history; for instance, the general recommendation is six months for a monthly publication, eight weeks for a weekly, or at least a few weeks through a daily or 24/7 web publication.

As you're reading, look for the kinds of sections that are included as regular features. What formats do they use? In a magazine, the standard set-up features a "front-of-book" section and sometimes also a "back-of-book" section (magazines are sometimes referenced as "the book" in industry jargon) with short newsy pieces, plus a "feature well" with two or three longer feature articles that delve into longer stories. For a newcomer (and an experienced writer who is a new freelancer, or an experienced freelancer who is new to a publication), shorter pieces are the best to try pitching, as editors are more inclined to take a risk on a new writer writing a shorter piece than a longer one. Writing for a new publication is sort of like a first date: they don't know you; you don't know them — on both sides, you're taking a risk that the other is a big bore with no table manners — in other words, that you're a writer who says they know how to write but can't string a sentence together. With editors, the challenge is even worse, as anyone can say they know grammar, but determining who knows grammar plus has all of the specialized knowledge of an experienced editor is hard to suss out — this is the reason for many editing tests and short starter assignments in the editing world.

In terms of who to pitch, the "masthead" is the place to look for names and titles of people who work at a publication in a print magazine. Roles at a magazine in descending order of rank include editor-in-chief, deputy editor, managing editor, senior editors, associate editors, and assistant editors. Your best bet is usually to pitch to a senior editor for a feature or an associate editor for a shorter front-of-book piece. Or for a particular type of story, there may be an obvious editor; for example, a food editor would be the best person to consider your pitch about new fall pumpkin recipes. You'll find the masthead in a list within the first five pages or so of a traditional magazine, usually somewhere near the editor's letter in a newspaper, and at the bottom of a publication's website (try looking under the About section). While you're on the magazine's website, look out for the writers' guidelines — some publications put together a totally handy guide on what the magazine looks for that can be gold in terms of figuring out where to send your pitch. Sometimes the "media kit," traditionally targeted toward advertisers, can also contain a lot of good information about the magazine's audience and demographics.

In a newspaper, look to see what sections are featured. While some sections are fairly standard, not every general newspaper will have every topic covered. For example, health stories are sometimes covered in a more general lifestyle section rather than in a dedicated health section. One niche I write in, careers, is covered in very few general publications, a fact that is very surprising to me when you consider that most of us spend at least eight hours a day at work.

You can also look for the phrase "special to" attached to the story, a tagline that indicates the story was written by a freelancer instead of a staff writer. Sometimes the word "freelancer" also appears directly in the "byline" (the line below the headline that says who wrote the story, or who it is by). This often signals that the section is more open to freelancers (unless it is regularly written by that "special to" author — another reason it's good to check several issues of the publication). If you have questions about which sections may be open to pitches, you can also try calling or emailing the magazine's editorial assistant (another title to get familiar with), who may be able to give you some basic information.

While I'm reviewing different types of publications, you should know that there is an entire range of publications that the average non-writer doesn't realize exists: trade publications. These serve specific industries, from manufacturing to professional services to agriculture. Unless you're a lawyer who reads *Canadian Lawyer* or a human-resources expert who reads *HR Professional*, you might never encounter these titles, but to their industries they can be very important sources of news. And to writers they can be a great source of work, as trade publishers are constantly in need of content. As you look for publications to pitch, be sure to see what industry or trade magazines serve your niche.

For all magazines, you'll also want to look at the kinds of stories that a publication prints and the tone that they use. For example, a fashion magazine that caters to a younger generation may use a less formal tone than one with an older readership, and a financial column might be written in a more conservative tone with fewer slang words and more technical jargon than a fashion magazine. When you look for story ideas and when you write your pitches, make sure to take these elements into account. Especially for your first pitches, your goal is to fit into the existing tone and approach of the magazine rather than to suggest something radically different. Taking a chance on a new writer who is also pitching an idea that's outside of their mainstream is just too far a stretch. If you can, go beyond the story topics to observe the types of stories the magazine publishes — are they investigative? Newsy? Gossipy? Do they write a lot of profiles or only cover companies using a feature story format with quotes? When pitching, try to think about how your story can fit these formats.

As you're looking through the publications to figure out what they publish, try to determine what their readership is like. Many magazines have a very specific audience, and their editors will only assign stories that appeal to that particular demographic. For example, one women's magazine might envisage their typical readers as women between the ages of thirty and fifty-five who are university educated, have at least two children, own their homes, and have been employed in the same job for many years. Another women's magazine might cater to women under thirty who are just settling into their careers, are renters, and do not have families but are actively dating. Thinking about the readership or audience profile of a magazine can help you decide if your story idea fits. You wouldn't want to pitch a story about "healthy school lunches for happy kids" to the younger women's magazine.

Lastly, you'll also want to make sure your timing is right for your chosen publication. Keep in mind that the average monthly publication is assembled at minimum four months in advance, so to get your time-sensitive story considered, approved, and written before that date, you might think about pitching six months or more ahead. This means that in August, the publication is already working on the Christmas issue, so your article on Christmas decorating should probably be pitched in the spring. On the flipside, a news website will be looking for stories tied to a tight timeline, so you'll have to move quickly both in pitching and writing the story to make it work. Timeliness can be a powerful selling factor, so if you find ideas that are tied to a specific time frame, make sure you convey that in your pitch, possibly even in the subject line: URGENT.

Becoming a reader of the types of work you'd like to write in that realm is also a good idea. While nobody ever grows up reading annual reports or sizzling email sequences, if those forms are produced by a company you'd like to write for, then it helps to familiarize yourself with them. Download three years of a company's annual reports and see what components are included. Do they highlight success stories through journalistic-style articles, or is it more of a uniform narrative by a single writer? What do the visuals tell you about the tone the company wants to convey? Download annual reports from a handful of different types of companies — a bank, a non-profit, and an arts organization — and consider the ways they are different and the same in terms of information featured, tone, and visuals. As with the magazines, think about who the target audiences might be for these forms. Repeat this exercise with as many forms as interest you. Social media can be an interesting one — look back through the past few weeks or months of an organization's feed. What can you discern about their strategy? Becoming a student of these forms can make you more qualified to pitch them and more able to field questions when a client asks if you are able to produce them. Yes, this business is a constant learning experience.

For those of you second-career writers who already have a decade of experience, I hope you are nodding at these approaches to finding story ideas and pitching publications. This information is likely not new to you, although you may be embracing the freedom of having multiple clients to pitch to instead of the limitations of a single workplace. Just a warning that the chapters on pitching and writing articles might be review for you, so feel free to skip to what's useful. Or if you're like me, feel free to read even more intently because it's fun to see how another writer approaches things.

Exercises

EXERCISE 1

Brainstorm five good story ideas that have come to your attention in the last month. They can either be articles you've read, something you've heard from a friend, or your own discoveries. What makes these ideas stand out? How do they fit criteria for what makes a good story idea?

EXERCISE 2

Think about one magazine or publication you're familiar with as a reader. Find a copy and look through it with your writer's hat on. Describe the sections in that publication. What do you think their audience profile looks like? See if you can find writers' guidelines or a media kit on their website. What do you think their editor would be looking for in a pitch? What is one idea you think would be a good fit for one of their shorter sections?

Chapter 5

The Art of the Pitch

Now that your business is set up, it's time to just sit back and wait for the phone to ring and your inbox to fill up with eager requests for your services.

Said no successful freelancer ever.

No matter how great your website looks and how lovely your business cards turn out, no matter how great a time you had at the networking event discovering all the things you have in common with a fellow writer or editor, at some point in order to make a living you're going to have to start selling yourself, and that proposition can be super awkward and uncomfortable. But the sooner you stop seeing it as fully ick, the quicker you can start actually making a living.

For careerists who have spent their entire career in-house and only now are pivoting to freelance, this moment might be when you lean in and perhaps cringe a bit. Remember those people who pitched you once in your fancy editorial job as a senior editor or internal communications specialist? You're them now. Don't worry, your long experience in knowing what a good story is and your established editorial judgment will stand you in good stead. Editors, this chapter is still not your wheelhouse, but seeing how a story comes to life before it comes to you may be of interest. Possibly you're curious to add writing to your own freelance business. Or feel free to flip to the chapter on pitching to corporate clients if you're itching to get started with your own outreach.

Whether you're pitching an idea that you'd like to write for a magazine or pitching yourself as a potential writer on a project, from a company newsletter to an annual report, your business depends on reaching out via email, picking up the phone, and doing ugly things like telling someone why they should assign you work and pay you good money to provide a service.

One way to overcome this fear is to flip it on its head. Think about the good you're doing by bringing a great idea to a stressed-out editor or by helping an overworked communications specialist rushed off her feet. If you truly believe you're the right writer or editor for the job, or you have the right idea for a magazine's readership, that fit will come across naturally in your enthusiasm and knowledge about the topic. Go you! Until then, it's "fake it 'til you make it." Or don't, which is the darker alternative, because inertia rarely results in much money.

Why Pitch?

Pitches, regardless of whether your target is a publication or an organization, are more common than they are different. If you're pitching to a publication, you're usually selling your idea plus yourself as the right writer. If you're pitching to a new client (see chapter 7), you're more focused on yourself and your experience in providing similar services for similar customers. Since pitches, or queries, are the main vehicle that new writers use to connect with magazines, they tend to be more templated than the "prospecting letters" or "letters of introduction" designed for client outreach. Most freelancers pitch themselves to work on everything from one-off assignments to support editorial to more formal recruitment opportunities, such as requests for proposals.

Now, once you've started to develop those essential relationships with editors and clients, it's likely you will get repeat business (yay!). You'll also get known in your community and start to gain referral business, either from clients who pass your name along or from colleagues who pass work along either because they don't have time or think your skills are a better fit. These are all great ways to get business, because the effort is relatively low compared to the pitching I'm about to get into (definitely thank the person who refers you with a grateful email or even small gift). Perhaps it's time to bring in some numbers from my mini survey of freelancers to note that "mostly referral and some pitching" was the top answer, at 37 percent, and "referral" was a close second, at 35 percent, to the question, "How do you find new work?" Referral and pitching came in in equal measure at 15 percent, followed by mentions such as "creating my own projects" and "online directories."

Yet despite the fun anticipation of repeat business and referrals, I never think it's that helpful to tell new writers I only get work by referral. To tell newcomers to "just get a network" is not particularly actionable. Also, even twenty years in, I still pitch! Because editors move, publications fold, and so do organizations. Budgets can dry up, new managers can haul in their favourite freelancer from their previous job, or they can also hire full-time staff to do the work previously outsourced to a freelancer. The great opening that you got when someone went on parental leave suddenly closes when they come back (true story). Eventually, you're going to need more clients than the handful you've started with, so why not keep reaching out and adding a few new ones every quarter?

Just a note about the fear element in pitching. Just because I embraced feisty as my adjective, that's not the same as loud. As a confirmed introvert, I have had to learn ways to become more comfortable with everything from cold pitching to public speaking. I guess I have started to value what those activities can bring to my business over the nerve that it takes to send a cold email. It took some practice, and I don't think I'll ever get to the place where it's my favourite activity, but seeing that it works makes me continue working at it.

Publication Pitch Elements

Once you've got your story idea, the perfect publication, and the ideal section, it's time to create your pitch or query letter. But first: scour your intended publication to make sure they haven't already written about it. I'd search back four to six months through a monthly and a few weeks through a weekly or daily. The search engine on the publication's website can be a useful tool. If you're pitching a major feature, you'll also want to check the competitor publications — if *Chatelaine* magazine recently published a splashy story on menopause, then *Canadian Living* magazine is likely at minimum to want a different angle — if you do find a story on your idea, the best approach is not to hide it but to reference it and show how your angle will be different.

Okay, so your search produced nothing and your idea is in the clear. Think of the pitch as a moment to distill all the information that the editor needs to greenlight your idea, but equally as an opportunity to show off your writing style. Most pitches should read like the opening of your proposed article, using narrative elements like character and anecdote and details like statistics and factoids that you will try to weave into the story itself. This is also the place to mention any possible timeliness factors, or reasons to do the story now (often called "the hook").

After settling on an idea, your pitch or query will move into nuts-and-bolts details about the story elements. Include any further details to thoroughly describe the story, interview suggestions, and possibly even structural notes to give the editor a sense of your proposed outline if it's a longer feature. Try to give a sense of the overall theme, if appropriate, especially if the story will speak to a wider issue that would be of interest to readers of that particular publication. A story about Mary's particular experience becomes an inroad to discussing the larger question of intimate partner violence.

In the next section, provide those important details about why you are the writer most suited to write the story: your experience with the topic and any specialized knowledge or connections you bring to the story. For example, if you're pitching a story about teaching abroad and you taught in Japan for two years, be sure to note that differentiator. Probably lead with it. End your pitch with a summary of your writing experience, links to your published articles, and information on how to follow up with you.

Pitches can range in length from two paragraphs to two pages, the latter being more common for a longer feature pitch. If you are starting out a new relationship with an editor, you should opt for a longer pitch, where you can explain elements in detail, although this format has been changing in recent years, as many editors prefer shorter pitches, full stop. So, if you have the opportunity to speak with someone who already writes for the publication, making that call can be a golden opportunity to ask what its particular editors go for. Also pay attention to any intel in the writers' guidelines.

As a short example, here's my pitch about the chickens I mentioned in an earlier chapter (I knew you'd be curious). This was for a short 300-word piece in the front-of-book section of a national general interest magazine:

> SUBJECT: PITCH: Adopting heritage hens to preserve chicken genetics
> Dear Editor:
> Babs and Henriette are elegant ladies who enjoy a sweet life in the sunshine hunting for food. Their beautiful appearance and quirky habits catch the attention of many caregivers, including

those who make sure they're fed and adoptive families who help to fund this upkeep. In return, their adoptive families get a dozen of the ladies' eggs to take home every two weeks. Yes, Babs and Henriette are chickens.

Part of a program at the University of Alberta to preserve vulnerable bloodlines of heritage hens, Babs and Henriette are just two of many chickens whose upkeep is paid for by donations from the public, in amounts ranging from $50 to $500. Adopters receive eggs, naming rights, and the chance to support this research. Although the project was initially launched as a way to raise the $75,000 needed to maintain coops for the residents of the U of A's Poultry Research Centre, two years later the project includes over 400 members and there is now a waiting list for chicken adoption. Here's the project's website: heritagechickens.ualberta.ca/.

In practical terms, the project preserves chicken genetics that are being out-bred by commercial strains, where the sole focus is on efficiency. Yet the project has also fostered a community around the hens (which recently won the university's community leader award). This is reflected on the project's Tumblr site at uofaheritagechicken.tumblr.com, where researchers share everything from adopters' naming stories to the details of their daily interactions with the chickens.

I think this would make a great 300-word piece for your "Miscellany" section (perhaps the setting at a university would also make it appropriate as a fall "back-to-school" story). I would like to interview the researchers behind the project as well as an adopter to find out about how the project works as both a tool for public education and a fun way to bring the community closer. Here's a press release about the initiative: ualberta.ca/folio/2015/05/chicken-adoption-program-hatches-free-range-learning.html.

I'm a freelance writer with over a dozen years of experience contributing articles to magazines and newspapers. My portfolio is online at suzannebowness.com. Please contact me if you have any questions, or to discuss moving forward with this story.

Thanks,

Sue

<my email signature>

As you'll notice, at approximately 350 words, this pitch is already longer than the intended article, but it contains the necessary details to sell the editor:

- an opening that shows off narrative writing, written in a playful tone with the description of ladies who turn out to be hens
- details about the project that the chickens represent and the larger problem that the research solves (that these bloodlines will die out if they're not preserved)
- specific details about who should be interviewed for the story
- details on where the story will fit in the publication
- additional hook with the back-to-school factor (possibly a stretch)
- reference to my portfolio and contact information

While longer pitches will get into sections and themes and provide more detail on why this story suits the readership, even in this shorter pitch, I've taken the time to cover all the essential elements.

You may be worried that your pitches won't land without any previous articles. That concern is legitimate, because editors are always worried about taking chances. Some of the best ways to overcome this uncertainty can be, as I mentioned previously, to pitch a story where you have special access (your grandmother wrote a song that became a one-hit wonder) or to consider smaller publications that pay less (maybe a community newspaper), where established writers will not be interested in pitching.

You can also try to create your first writing samples by starting your own blog and writing a couple of pieces on a volunteer basis so that you have published samples (I share this suggestion reluctantly as I don't want writers writing for free, but when starting out it can be necessary — just trade up to paid work as soon as you can). You can also focus your pitch mostly on the idea and less on your nonexistent writing samples, although I'd at least create a LinkedIn profile to show an editor that you exist professionally, and try to write some posts or samples — something for potential editors and clients to read that shows off your writerly sass.

One last caveat here is that in spite of your zeal for publication, no story is worth ruining your relationships, livelihood, or safety — I had a student who wanted to write an exposé on the lousy restaurant that she worked for as a server, and I asked, "Do you want to work there still?" "Yes, I need the job." Then don't jeopardize that job until you have a different one. And especially don't tackle hard topics that may cause you pain for your first assignment, which may already be difficult enough given the learning curve.

Pitching Process

Email is almost universally the form by which editors want to receive pitches, although yes, I've definitely heard of successful pitching via tweet or direct message. But where possible, you need to find both the right editor and the correct contact information to reach these contacts directly.

Often, different editors handle each part of the magazine; as I mentioned in an earlier chapter, an assistant or associate editor will generally handle front-of-book pitches, whereas a senior editor usually handles features. The editor-in-chief or deputy editor is usually more involved with the management of the magazine, except in the case of a smaller magazine, where they may well be the person to pitch directly. Avoid pitching the info@publication.com address, since these are checked infrequently and often by interns who don't have a lot of assigning power. And use "Pitch" in the subject line, as in the sample pitch above (PITCH: Adopting heritage hens to preserve chicken genetics), and include the pitch in the body of your email.

Generally, do not expect to hear back immediately about your pitch, but feel free to send a follow-up email a week or two later if you haven't heard back (you can send it sooner if the story is very timely). Follow up again a couple of weeks after that follow-up, and perhaps once more.

After a couple of emails, you could also try calling the editor on the phone, although many hate phone calls, so see how far you can get with email first (especially now that many editors are working from home, numbers on websites may no longer be valid). Once you are on the phone, try to be succinct and direct in your follow-up — ditto with any voicemail you may leave.

Many editors will get back to you even with a rejection, but if you haven't heard from the editor, you should probably assume you can move on to another market. I hate this part of the process (rejection sucks, no matter where you are in your career), but it happens. As you move on, you may want to send one more email and tell the lousy scoundrel that you're taking your story elsewhere. Wait a day, then do so.

When rejection happens, either outright or passively via the "wall of silence," you and your idea are once again free agents. Even before a rejection, I try to brainstorm backup markets so that I can quickly turn the pitch around — of course, you'll need to tinker with it so it fits the next publication's tone and approach — and address it to a new editor.

While tempting, avoid pitching to multiple publications at the same time. This is a bit unfair to freelancers, given that editors sometimes take their time in responding, but simultaneous pitching is still fairly taboo. If you have an idea that is genuinely timely, you may make an exception, but in that case you should clearly state that the pitch is a simultaneous submission and you will let the editor know immediately about interest from elsewhere. Follow through on that promise to maintain your integrity.

Once you do get your pitch accepted by a publication, the editor will generally send you an assignment letter. This can be as informal as a short email telling you to go ahead with your pitch as outlined, or a more detailed, page-length assignment letter outlining the elements of your pitch that the editor would like you to focus on (they may call you to discuss these) and any additional contacts they would like you to make.

In the assignment letter, editors should confirm elements like payment, word count (how many words they would like you to submit), deadline, and any additional details. Chapter 8 has more details on what to look for in these letters.

A note about pitching for magazines specifically: you should know that there are certain magazines that every writer would love to write for (hello, *New Yorker*, *Atlantic*, *Walrus*), and just like you, even seasoned writers who may have assignments rolling in from other publications are still writing their wing-and-a-prayer pitches to those dream publications. I am always torn about encouraging my students to pitch to these as their first publication, since the chances of acceptance are likely lower given how many people want to get in there, but at the same time a great idea is a great idea, and a newcomer still has as good a chance at sliding into home base with one of those. So, I usually tell students that I'm not going to crush their dreams if they really do want to pitch to *Chatelaine* magazine on their first attempt (memorably, a student did and landed a nice meaty feature based on a personal angle even before graduation — impressive). But why not also pitch to some other lower-paying, frequently publishing, youthful magazines where they might have a better chance of an early win? Again, the choice is theirs (yours), and mine is just a friendly warning.

Which also raises the issue that not every pitch will be to your dream magazine or dream client. If we spent all our time pitching to the *New Yorker* and getting no assignments, then we wouldn't have a business. So usually, you need to find a mix of dream publications and more accessible bread-and-butter publications and workaday clients, ones that pay the bills and where you say, "At least I'm writing" and "At least I'm getting paid *something*." But save those Friday afternoons for the occasional dream pitch or project. You'll live your best life when you're keeping an eye on both your business and writing ambitions.

Exercises

EXERCISE 1

Think of a new trend you've noticed, gossip you've heard recently, or that long-standing story that's been rolling around in your head for years — many writers have one. Without censoring yourself, write out the idea as you would tell it to a friend. What makes you most excited about it? What could you learn by researching it, and what do you think your readers would love about it? Can you think of a publication to pitch it to?

EXERCISE 2

Take your newly written story idea and revisit it through the lens of pitching. Can you think of how you would shape it to include

- an opening that shows off narrative writing,
- details about the idea that provide a concrete sense of why the story is important,
- specific details about who should be interviewed for the story,
- details on where the story will fit in your imagined publication, and
- any timeliness factors?

Does your pitch need more research? If so, do it! If not, try writing it using the format I've discussed in this chapter. Send it? Send it!

Chapter 6

How to Write an Article

Freelancing can cover a wide range of writing, from articles to grants to proposals to social media posts. In chapter 2, I looked at the types of writing you could pursue and discussed the pros and cons of becoming a generalist or a specialist writer with a niche focused on a particular sector, content type, or both. As a freelancer, you may well work on a variety of writing types, as well as on editing, project management, and other adjacent tasks. But there may be certain types of writing that you return to again and again, either because they become your favourites, or you get good at them, or they are in demand, or all of the above.

For me, this form has been the article, and I think it's useful to learn for a few reasons. First, with many journalistic publications out there looking for ideas, the article is a more accessible form to the newcomer because there's already a market. While it may be hard to guess what some organizations need, the magazine or newspaper or website will always need articles, and because back issues are available for you to examine, you can figure out what type and length and style of articles they want, and suddenly (with effort) you'll find yourself with a paid assignment.

Many organizations also need articles for their blogs and newsletters, and even annual reports are more magazine-like, as they celebrate success stories with journalistic-style stories. In the nonprofit world, writers use journalistic storytelling to create strong narratives in their fundraising materials and celebrate donors through stories. The last few annual reports I've written have been all journalistic-style articles telling the stories of people inside the organization. So, it's a useful form in many niches, one that can take you through many freelance opportunities. Plus, it's fun.

So how do you do it?

Let's assume that you pitched your fantastic idea from the previous chapter, that idea was accepted, and you have the green light to create an article. Often, your editor will give you an assignment letter or creative brief that outlines what should go into the article. If you wrote the pitch, the assignment letter (read: email) may contain part or most of your idea and any added elements that your editor might want covered. Depending on the editor and also the complexity of the story, the assignment letter might be shorter or longer than an email — for features, a good editor will provide a page or two describing what to include in the story and even some sources to contact. Ideally the editor will give you a word count, a deadline, and a sense of what they want you to accomplish with the story. Word counts for smaller articles can run from 250 to 500 words; for medium-length articles, 500 to 800 words; and for feature articles, from 1,000 to 3,500 words. Some longer feature stories in magazines can run over 5,000 words, although those assignment lengths are becoming scarcer.

With added length, your article may be more complex, so your deadline should be longer. For a shorter article, expect two to three weeks; for a medium-length article, it would be nice to have three to four weeks; and for a longer feature, you should ask for four to six weeks. For more involved stories, like a 5,000-word investigation for

Toronto Life magazine, you may get several months and expect to talk to two dozen sources. Deadlines should also depend on how many sources you're expected to include in the story, because interviewing means that you need to wait for sources to get back to you, then you can schedule, conduct, and incorporate the interviews into your draft. For a shorter piece, you may need only one or two interviews, whereas for a longer piece, you may need seven or eight or even more.

If your editor is in a rush, they may ask for a shorter deadline, so it's a balance between feeling confident to ask for more time and accommodating clients if the request is a bit tight but manageable. You can also charge a rush fee for work with an unreasonable timeline, but often I only add this charge if it's really inconvenient (read: weekend work) and mostly just for corporate clients. Regardless of the deadline you accept, you should still make sure you can complete the work in that time frame. Be real with yourself and with your client.

Making a Plan

Now that you have the assignment, you need to figure out how it fits in your own schedule. Start by putting the deadline in your calendar. Then make, mentally or otherwise, a "workback schedule" — a list of interim deadlines broken down week by week until the final deadline — to help you stay on track. For example, if you have a one-month deadline for a 1,200-word article, your schedule might look like this:

- Week 1: research and reach out to interviewees
- Week 2: start interviewing and create outline based on research
- Week 3: write first draft plus finish up any late interviews
- Week 4: write second draft, edit, proofread, and send

Your workback schedule can be somewhat flexible, but it should keep you on track to meet your final deadline. The most important task is the one most outside your control: reaching out to interviewees. Without invitation, you're reaching out to interrupt their lives to ask them for twenty to thirty minutes that they didn't expect to give up until your email arrived. Whether they're a busy CEO, or university professor, or university student, or mother of four, you've given prospective interviewees something extra to juggle. There's going to be some back and forth to fit your interview into their schedule, and you have to fit their schedule into yours. Maybe they're on vacation in week two so cannot speak until week four, but if you find out about those parameters in week one, then you can work around their timelines or find another interviewee. That's why you need to reach out as soon as you can. Don't procrastinate — a month sounds like a long time, but it's really not.

But hold on, before all of that, you need to figure out who you will interview.

Not only do you want to think about the people you need to tell the story you promised to deliver, but you need to think about pulling together the right mix of people. Most stories have a central figure or handful of people who are experts in the subject, either by lived experience or by education. Your editor may ask you to interview specific people and you should abide by that. You'll also want to ensure representation in your story so that it doesn't just speak for one gender or racial group or age, unless that's the purpose (and even then, consider the benefits of extra representation). If you write a feature for a national magazine, you should think about soliciting interviewees from across the country.

Any writer should be thinking about gender representation as well as diversity representation, i.e., interviewing people from different races, and any other diversity factor relevant to your story. When I'm writing an article for a university magazine, I'm trying to make sure that I interview a first-year student as well as an upper-year student and one in science and one in arts. If I'm writing an article that argues a perspective, I want to get the opposite perspective into the story as well. If it's a national magazine, you'll want geographic diversity in interviewees from coast to coast to coast. If this need for comprehensive coverage seems stressful, rest assured that you won't be able to fit in all representations. But you'll look pretty insensitive if you write a story on a general topic where you only interview men, unless there's a good reason. And there usually isn't. So, unless you're writing for a young women's magazine where it makes sense to speak mostly to young women, or for a city magazine where the experts would naturally be urban dwellers, keep representation goals in mind, and you'll get a better, fairer story that incorporates more perspectives and demographics.

Final tip: remember to have a couple of spare interviewee possibilities in mind as backup in case any of your interviews fall through or people never get back to you.

Interviewing

Once you make up your list of interviewees, you should reach out to them right away. Day one. Send interviewees an email identifying yourself as a freelancer (you can leave out the "feisty" just this one time), the publication or organization you're writing for, the article topic and why you think they'll be a great source (a little demure flattery never hurts), your deadline, and the amount of time you will need for the interview. Sometimes you'll reach out to a media relations or PR professional whose job it is to put you in touch with the actual interviewee. These people can be great to have on your side, a nice shortcut to other information about the organization. Keep in mind that PR folks are hired by the organization they represent, so part of their job is to ensure that only positive stories are written, and they will steer you in the direction of all the amazing things their company has done, when you may want to write a more balanced story. But overall, they are someone you want to make your friend, as they can save you time in coordinating and granting access to busy interview subjects.

When you do reach the person who you will interview, I often suggest to the media relations professional that I'm happy to schedule directly with the interviewee or their assistant, which skips a middle person. Once you are communicating with the calendar-keeper, suggest a timeframe that will be sufficient to ask your questions but doesn't waste their time — usually twenty to thirty minutes for an expert and forty-five minutes for a profile or main source. Suggest a platform — video conferencing is popular, or the phone. Pro tip: when you state your deadline, don't give interviewees the REAL deadline, tell them a couple of days earlier (insider tip: your editor has probably done this with your assignment deadline; respect their deadline even though you know this secret — timeliness is important for making a good impression on an editor). Here's a sample note to schedule an interview:

> Dear INTERVIEWEE,
> I'm a freelance writer assigned to write an article about you for MAGAZINE/COMPANY. I'm writing to set up an interview time. My deadline is FAKE DEADLINE, 2 DAYS BEFORE REAL DEADLINE, and I would need to have about 20–30 minutes of your time over the phone or Zoom. Would an interview be possible for next week? Please let me know some days and times that work. I look forward to speaking with you!
>   Thanks,
>   Sue

In the past year, I've adopted a digital calendar app; I send interviewees an optional link to it to book their own time. While I hesitated to try this approach, afraid that interviewees would be put out by this ask, the general response has been to use it, saving me a ton of time with scheduling back and forth.

A word about email interviewing: avoid. You will want to, because it's so easy and you don't have to work up the nerve to get on the phone, and you can hide behind the keyboard. But it results in The. Worst. Interviews. After all, if someone asks you for your opinion on something, and you have to write an essay about it and you have a bunch of other stuff to do, how much time and effort are you going to put into your reply? So, try to get the person on the phone or on video conference, where you can ask follow-up questions and engage in a conversation. Even nicer is in person, where you can note a person's body language and the setting or even see the interviewees in their natural habitat at home or work — great for profiles where possible.

With the pandemic rise of video conferencing, people have become a lot more comfortable over these platforms, so many interviewees request it (sometimes insisting on their own more secure workplace platforms) and even feel comfortable when you ask to record the interviews (on Zoom, when you click the record button, Zoom's robot voice automatically states that a recording is in progress, forcing the interviewee to acknowledge it). Check the legal requirements on recording interviews; in some places, consent is required from only one person on the call but in others both parties need to agree. I tell everyone that I'm recording for my notes. The only downside here is, of course, you need to be camera-ready (at least from the waist up), more so than when interviews were mostly done over the phone.

After all, an interview is just that: a scheduled conversation. You'll come up with your set of seven or eight questions, which you should try to resist asking firing-squad style. If the interviewee answers question four when you were about to ask question two, just go with it. Start with a softball question, likely something factual; for example, if you're profiling the interviewee as CEO of a start-up, ask them about the education and career path that led to that position. This info is easy for them, so they'll start to relax. People like to talk about themselves and will start to ramble and maybe answer questions seven and three along the way. As they answer, just let the interviewee talk, unless they really are rambling, in which case gently steer them back to a question they haven't yet answered.

Once the interviewee is relaxed and in a groove, then you can hit them with something more hardball, like what their philosophy is on business or if they have thought about how their start-up infringes on users' privacy rights. Asking these tougher questions at the end also has the benefit that if your interviewee storms off (or the phone equivalent), you've already completed most of the interview. If they sidestep a question or provide a weak answer, try to think of a different way to ask it; for example, the question about business philosophy can also be reframed: Which business gurus do they admire, and what philosophies do they incorporate into their own venture? While most adults will not realize they are answering the same question, be prepared that children will call you out. "You already asked me that!" said an adorable girl the time I was hanging out by a sandbox collecting quotes for a feature in a private-school magazine. Kindergarteners are the worst.

As you're asking all these questions, you're also doing a bunch more things: you're listening and absorbing their answers, you're thinking about your follow-up questions, you're thinking about what questions on your list you still need to ask, you're thinking about the time limit you have (you can't talk for an hour if you only asked for twenty minutes), and you're thinking about whether your recorder is working. That's another pro tip: record all your conversations. I am a fast typist after twenty-plus years of writing articles, but I cannot type at the speed of a fast talker and neither can you.

A recording will take a bit of the pressure off so that if you don't get everything down, you will still be able to capture fuller quotes and sentences that make your story sound better.

We're lucky now that artificial intelligence has entered the transcription world, so you don't even need to worry about taking the time to transcribe your interviews manually (warning: AI transcriptions are still crap, so you really have to carefully review the quotes you will use — I have read AI transcripts that literally put swear words into the mouths of children). Also, recording technology has become really easy on video platforms like Zoom, and phone apps are useful too (although I still occasionally use my digital recorder beside a phone on speaker mode).

Fast forward to your completion of five to eight successful interviews brimming with usable quotes, several pages of research and notes, and a head spinning with ideas for your feature. You're almost at the writing part. Now you need to take all of the information swirling around and start cobbling it into a readable feature. Given that there are infinite approaches, how do you get started?

Writing

You get started writing any way you can. If you're lucky, there may have been a moment in one of your interviews where someone related an anecdote so interesting, made a comment so thought-provoking, or worded something so perfectly that you know it will become your opening. I'm glad nobody can see me on phone interviews at these zen moments because I have the DUMBEST grin on my face as I think to myself THAT'S IT. If you're not lucky to have this moment (and it's fairly rare), I go back to my story assignment, or even to what I originally pitched, and ask, "What question was I trying to answer and what was the most pertinent or maybe the most unexpected thing I heard?" Since openings are the most difficult to write, I almost never try to write them first unless they dropped from the sky (see: zen moment), so I try to think about the different types of things people said and think about how I can group quotes by topic. For example, if an article is a report on an event, a chronological organization might be most logical. If you're stuck, you can also try a couple of different structures and see which works best.

Whatever you do, try not to just stare at a blank page. Instead, put what you think you have in an order that makes sense to you, and most importantly, will make sense to the reader. Think about how you'll structure the article — by topic? Chronologically? By most important to least important topic? Create an outline by topic, and under each topic, list different research bits, quote ideas, and points you want to make. Move the topics around (I like to colour code by topic or sometimes even by interviewee, which is easy to do in programs like Word, where you can colour your fonts) into the order you think makes the most sense for the reader (again, try not to overthink it). Then start writing the topic that comes most easily to you. Writing begets writing. Do NOT try to start from the beginning and come up with the perfect opening. After you've written, even roughly, go to the next easiest section. Soon you will start making connections and thinking about elements to add to your lists by topic and the story will emerge. If you are approaching any kind of momentum, DO NOT STOP. You probably shouldn't reschedule interviews, but if you had a plan to work on this article for an hour and then hit the gym, DO NOT HIT THE GYM. DO NOT WALK THE DOG. Respect the flow.

If you are having the opposite experience, and each section seems as hard as the last, then do go to the gym when scheduled. Once you are partway into your story, your back burner brain will take over a bit, and you'll think about the way the quote about so-and-so belongs in section B, not in A. And hey, wasn't there a study that confirmed what interviewee 2 said? You'll probably come up with your opening in the shower or just before bed (keep that notebook or notes app handy in your nightstand). If it still doesn't come, then plan another session, trying to write the next easiest section. Soon you will have something manageable. To recall the wisdom of writer Anne Lamott in her well-known book *Bird by Bird*, take it paragraph by paragraph and then try to improve it in the revisions.

Building the Article

For the rest of the article, try to keep the reader in mind as you structure it — include your background and context at the start so readers feel grounded enough to understand the rest of the article. Build your structure in a way that best suits the subject matter, ideally moving between topics with transitional sentences that help the reader know what they'll read next. These can be as simple as, "Now let's take a look at what these best restaurants have in common" and "Restaurants may be fun, but running them can be expensive" — with each of these topic sentences, you can probably guess the content ahead. As you write, it will become clearer what topics flow best into the next. Don't hesitate to move sections around and try different organizational approaches (if I'm making a major change structurally, I sometimes save it as a new version so I can go back to the previous one if my "fabulous new approach" turns disastrous). Weave in statistics, anecdotes, and quotes in ways that keep the reader engaged and offer variety and readability, all while still working to build on the thesis that you included in the early paragraphs.

For newcomers, a word on sourcing in articles: you may notice when you scan your local newspaper article that it's usually not clogged with footnotes and references. For academic types, that habit can be hard to shake, but in mainstream articles, you have to cover credit in the text. If you quote from a study, start by noting the name and origins of the study in your introductory sentence — for example, "In a website article by the Canadian Women's Foundation on the gender pay gap, AUTHOR NAME says …" Try to include the publication or source, plus the author's name, plus the date. This can turn into a long sentence, but it's worth it. Also, when you're quoting an interviewee, start by introducing them with relevant bio details, such as their full name and organization. For example, "In *The Feisty Freelancer*, author and freelance writer Suzanne Bowness says …" As in all your academic essays, if the quote is directly from the interview, put it in quotes, and if you're summarizing their ideas, then paraphrase (still include your introductory phrase about the interviewee). Feel free to just use their name (usually the last name) on your second reference, so a paraphrase might read, "Bowness says don't plagiarize or you'll never be hired again as a freelancer."

Write and write and edit and edit. Then soon enough, you'll have something rough, but it actually looks like an article! Woohoo! Then onto the second draft, which is painful in some ways but so much less so than that first birthing. Give yourself some time between first and second draft, ideally a couple of days, but at minimum overnight. Some things I try to think about with the second draft: Did I fulfill my assignment? Did I tell the story I wanted to tell? Do I use all my sources well? (Not equally — some sources may be more relevant or say smarter things; in fact, you may need to leave out any duds altogether.) Did I include an opposing viewpoint if relevant? (Not all stories need that; if you're writing about a hate crime, feel free to leave out the other side.) Did I capture the overall opinions of my sources? Does my organizational flow make logical sense and is it easy for the reader to understand? Are there any places where the reader would benefit from more background information to understand my narrative? Does my story argue a point or have a thesis? For example, if I'm writing an in-depth story, a feature, that argues the need for better accessibility on city streets, a statement declaring that argument should appear early in the story. For a 300-word front-of-book article, you may only have enough room to report the news rather than make a statement.

Breaking for Jargon

There are a few must-haves in an article that are most useful to talk about using the vocabulary that journalists use. Your headline and subhead are sometimes called "hed" and "dek," respectively, in journalism jargon. The opening of the article is generally referred to as the "lead" or "lede" and is typically a bit of storytelling, classically an anecdote, surprising statistic, or some other gem that draws the reader in to become interested in the story. That takes up the first paragraph or three, depending on the length of the feature (if it's a 300-word story, it's the first sentence). Then, within the first few paragraphs is the thesis statement that I mentioned above, where you tell the reader what you're going to be talking about for the rest of the story. The statement shouldn't be so textbook that it jars the reader but just orients them to the point you'll be making through the story.

Sometimes that thesis is contained within a paragraph that journalists refer to as the "nut graph" or "nut graf" (newspaper editors misspell words sometimes so they don't accidentally leave a note to the journalist in the copy, but instead it gets caught by spellcheck; also, graph/graf is short for paragraph), which provides more context for the thesis and story "in a nutshell." The best way to see these terms in action is to read a few feature stories and challenge yourself to identify the type of lede, the nut graf, and the thesis. It's always amusing when my students have just taken the class where they learn these terms (especially when someone else has taught it so I'm not expecting it) and they show up spouting jargon and all sounding like wizened journalists forty years into their careers.

Final Checks

Once you've identified big-picture items like thesis statement, solid structure, and organization, here are a few smaller elements to consider. Did you fully identify your interviewees, referencing them on the first instance by Firstname Lastname, occupation or reason for being in your story, and location if relevant? You can also add physical description if relevant, although be careful to leave out if not relevant, and identify race or gender *only* if relevant (don't note, for example, a female doctor or identify a Chinese banker unless that detail is highly relevant). Did you check your quotes against the audio to make sure they're correct and not inaccurately transcribed by AI? Did you add appropriate tags, like "said" or "says," to identify the quotes? And make sure that any ideas and wordings from others are credited (even accidental plagiarism is a major career killer)? Did you take a look at all your sections to make sure they move smoothly into one another instead of abruptly shifting? Did you include a proposed title/headline and subhead (hed and dek) — it is a standard courtesy to participate in this challenging element, even if your editor ultimately goes with something else. Did you quickly fact-check the name spellings of interviewees, company names, and locations (citing these facts correctly is such an easy win that fact-checking is worth the time, especially when we have the blessing of the internet at our fingertips). Have you read and reread the story? And read and reread and read and reread. Have you looked for any run-on sentences or grammar errors? Have you run the spell-checking program on your computer?

If so, then you might be finished. Your editor is not looking for a perfect draft; they're looking for your best first effort. So don't worry. If your story generally answers the question posed in the assignment, is in on deadline, and within 20 percent of the assigned word count, you're probably good. Congratulations. Go buy or make yourself a fancy coffee to celebrate and move on to your next assignment.

And now, it's time to turn to corporate client outreach, so you can expand your writing world even beyond magazines.

Exercises

EXERCISE 1

Find a magazine article that you've read recently and create a reverse outline, either mentally or by printing it out and annotating each paragraph. Look at how the writer opens the story, identify the nut graf, and think about the structure. Identify the sections that the writer has used and study how the writer transitions between them. What other literary techniques does the writer use, like imagery, scene, metaphor, or character?

EXERCISE 2

Think about the story you wanted to tell as you drafted your pitch. How would you write that story? What might be a good structure? Are there any other articles you've read that might be a good inspiration? Write an outline of that possible article, and get concrete about the kind of research and interviewing you would need to do to make it come to life.

THE FEISTY FREELANCER

© Iva Cheung

Chapter 7

Pitching Corporate Clients

Now that you are an expert at pitching and writing articles, you are set for your career as a freelance journalist. Except bad news: it's really difficult to make an adult living solely by writing articles for publication. With rates that haven't increased in forever (literally since the 1970s, says freelance writer Ann Douglas, author of the Mother of All Books Series) and a news landscape that is shrinking by the year, many writers choose to reach out to corporate clients as well. By corporate, I'm including anyone that isn't a magazine or newspaper but that needs editorial services, from large companies in every sector to educational institutions, to small businesses, to non-profits. Some freelancers may object to the term "corporate," especially if they're actively trying to avoid working for big, faceless corporations, but I'm using the term as a catch-all to indicate organizations that clearly use writing and editing but aren't known for it as their primary purpose in the same way as publications. We're living in a text-based world with needs from crafting emails to creating annual reports, newsletters, and social media posts. Opportunities abound!

Just to check in with my informal freelancer survey crew on the balance of income earned doing corporate work compared with income earned through journalism, only 7.5 percent reported they made a living with journalism writing alone (another 7.5 percent said three-quarters of their work came from journalism). Just over 26 percent said they earned all their income from corporate clients; another 28 percent said that half their income came from corporate clients, half from journalism. And I fall in with the remaining 30 percent, earning 25 percent of my income from journalism work and 75 percent from corporate work, with the latter increasing in the past decade. Of course, by corporate work, I mean often the same work I did for publications, namely writing articles, but now they're for non-publishing organizations.

Before delving into the client-pitching process, it's helpful to know what kinds of projects you can pitch. That depends on a potential client pool's budgets, needs, and content output. As I mentioned in my musings on choosing a niche, you should explore the types of content the company tends to publish as a way of figuring out what you could realistically write for them. In the technology industry, companies need a variety of forms to help sell their products, including sell sheets, case studies, and white papers. Non-profits need grants written and edited and fundraising letters crafted. Many large organizations of all types require annual reports for reporting purposes or other reports and brochures to highlight their work. Companies of all types, including small- and medium-sized businesses, need website copy, emails, and blog posts to help clearly describe and sell their services. Many organizations also need a steady flow of social media posts.

So, make notes about the types of content that organizations tend to produce and how often. The companies that produce more content may naturally need support in creating it. You can identify their output in part by what you see the organizations producing.

For example, your local hospital may put out an annual report, several news releases each month, a fundraising campaign quarterly, and emails that fly between their senior team like ping pong balls across a table. Someone is writing (and editing!) all of those texts. To provide an example from my own career, realizing I enjoy writing that involves interviewing people and structuring articles that bring their stories to life, I looked for niches that produce longer-form articles and found one in the magazines and blog posts produced by the higher-education sector. They use long-form content to accomplish the goal of keeping in touch with alumni (and their sweet, sweet donor dollars), celebrating their students, connecting with prospective students, and getting their academic research out into the world. Texts they produce include alumni magazines, blog posts for their websites, donor campaigns, impact reports to highlight the significance of their research (often through storytelling), as well as annual reports. Many universities are also large enough to have a magazine per faculty or several reports over a year.

Another market you could identify might be the small-business community in your city. You could even go smaller than that market and focus on start-ups in a tech-focused city or service-based businesses, such as accounting and law firms. Again, do your research to see if the market is big enough and whether they seem to produce regular writing. Do your potential start-up clients send regular sales emails? Do they post social media content? Do they have a newsletter or is there potential for one? All of these questions are useful in determining whether a market has enough prospective projects. Also try to find out if other freelancers are serving their needs (and, of course, whether they have an internal team). Like any start-up (that's you as an early freelancer), you're trying to do enough research to make an educated guess on whether a market is viable, meaning that there are enough players who need to outsource enough work (and that the market is not saturated with other freelancers and that they pay decently). So, research online what you can, talk to other freelancers in the niche if you can, and start your outreach. And if it doesn't work, pivot to your next best niche.

When you're starting out, don't expect to write or edit an annual report as your first assignment. Like publications, a company that takes a chance on a new writer will often give a newbie a small assignment to see if their writing is a fit; say, one blog post or a social post, and then assign more work later. That is, they'll assign you more work as long as you're as great as you claim to be, plus you meet your deadline, plus you are pleasant to work with (always be pleasant to work with). Eventually, clients may assign you a batch of blog posts (say, five or six), or a series of articles, or reward your diligence on the 1,000-word case study by inviting you to take on the 4,000-word white paper. They may even refer you to a colleague for their next case study or batch of blog posts. Unlike publications where you pitch, the ideas for these pieces most often come from the internal team, and you are tasked with the writing, often with a detailed outline called a "creative brief," which is like an assignment letter, and occasionally with interviews that they have lined up for you internally (for example, to interview the head of a department about a new company initiative for an article in their annual report). When you do corporate work, it is mostly also without a byline (the piece doesn't have your name on it), and the company owns the work (unlike work for publications, you're not associating the work with your byline, so it doesn't have the same reputational impact). You can still point to the work in your portfolio, although for complete peace of mind, you can check with the client as to whether they're fine with you including the work as samples.

As an editor reaching out for corporate work, you're also looking for evidence that the client buys what you're selling. Since the editor operates in the background, it can be harder to tell who needs editing work, but it is still possible to reach out within niches. Unlike writing, where you can easily share bylined samples on your website (obtain permission first if it's internal or unbylined work), editing experience is not as demonstrable, so it may be harder to provide samples (once you've worked with clients, you can ask them for permission to share samples of their edited documents, although as you can imagine some may be shy about their "before" texts). I've always found pitching editing more difficult than pitching writing, and it can often require more referrals. I've found it easier to stay within an editing niche; for example, most of my editing work has been for magazines or on corporate reports for think-tanks or non-profits, or I am copy editing and proofreading these same documents.

So how do you get yourself some of that sweet corporate writing and editing pie? With a little hustle to start.

Researching an Industry

To begin building a clientele, you need to figure out who your client is and how to reach them. Ideally you've chosen a niche with not only publications but also other organizations to target. In some ways, this industry research can be a challenge because it can be hard to know which potential clients might assign a lot of work to freelancers versus which firms handle most work in-house. Or even which companies create much output — I know my local contractor and mechanic do not need to spend a lot of time writing blog posts in order to be fairly busy most of the time. Or maybe they do — one client of mine in the last decade had a great lawn-care business that stood out because of his solid website and effort on social media.

One way to find out whether an industry is good to write for is to ask other freelancers already servicing that industry, maybe in a different geographic area. The downside is that these people are also your competitors, so you'll want to be tactful in your approach. Hey, why not give me all your clients!

Another approach is to try prospecting widely and see what comes of it. This is a long-term project for your business, best done on a consistent basis that also fits around deadlines already on your calendar. When I want to explore a new market, I generally try to build myself a little database of contacts within that industry. You could also do an informational interview with someone in that industry to get a sense of the kinds of publications they produce. Ask a lawyer which newsletters they subscribe to and what their firm puts out, or ask a banker friend how they find out about the latest new technology or what sorts of communications their company produces.

Say I was a health freelancer, and I decided to try hospitals as my first target, since in my initial research I had identified several hospitals in my city that seemed to publish reports regularly. I would try creating a list of as many area hospitals as I could find, sourced through Google, word of mouth, and any online directories that might be available. Then I would search the websites of these institutions and try to find a contact in the communications departments. Communications Manager or Communications Director are good job titles to approach. You could also consider reaching out to more than one contact; for example, a communications manager and a director of public relations may both hire writer/editors. At a university, both the communications department and the alumni relations department hire writers for different purposes, so I've found it worthwhile to send an email to each department. Also, at some universities, communications are decentralized, so it may be worth emailing the point person in each faculty.

If I didn't see a contact, I would call reception and try to find out this contact information directly (remember, people no longer like the phone, so this could be challenging). Similar to magazines, avoid sending an email to general "info@mailbox" as those tend not to be checked often. Add all your contacts to a spreadsheet (I use Excel or Google Sheets), and set goals for yourself on how many contacts you would like to reach out to per week. If you don't have any work, your job is doing this outreach to get work, so you may approach lots of contacts to start with, then fewer per week as you get busy. In my spreadsheet, I use columns like DATE/NAME/ CONTACT/EMAIL/PHONE/APPROACH/FOLLOWUP1/ FOLLOWUP2 to keep track of my efforts. If I do hear from a potential client, I keep detailed notes on what was said and when I can follow up. If I don't hear from someone, I put NR (for No Reply) in the approach column and stare at the spreadsheet, fuming for a couple of minutes, before deciding when to follow up. Today, there are great apps for organizing your client outreach that allow you to create reports or sort by particular demographics. I'm just referencing the spreadsheet method to emphasize that it can be this simple.

As another example, say you want to work as a grant writer for non-profits in your city. Make a list of the non-profits. In this world, another lead is the list of awards published by many granting agencies — look at these to identify organizations that received the awards. For example, theatres and publishers are funded by organizations such as the Canada Council, or local charities might receive city funds designated for municipal community projects. Since grant writing is a specific skill with very templated forms (fundraising letters, grants), they will probably want to see that you've done this type of work before they assign you their work, so you will want to make sure you have the skills (take a course or read books in this specialty area) before you approach them, or maybe develop some samples if you don't have any. You might even volunteer to write grants for a charity you love to get started in this niche and do your outreach after you have some samples ready.

The same goes for the editing world — as you are reaching out, especially to organizations where editing is central to their business, like publishers, prepare for your potential client to ask you to take an editing or proofreading test. Consider taking a course or brushing up your skills to bring them to the level needed to offer professional services (an English major with good grammar isn't enough — professional editing is more than catching typos). An editor colleague recently mentioned that applicants who submit resumés to her publisher go through a rigorous process to determine if they truly have the skills to do the work to the publisher's standards. If you're editing for an organization, they may not have a test but will try you out on a smaller piece to see what you come back with.

Once you have the contact information for your list of organizations, there are a couple of possible approaches. You could send an email to the potential client. You could call and try to get clients on the phone (it is helpful to write yourself a short script). Or you could do a combination, sending an email and following up with a phone call or vice versa, with the caveat that nobody likes to be followed up on the phone. I end up leaving a message, but it is still a way to cut through. That said, I'm a bit phone-phobic myself, so 95 percent of my cold outreach has been by cold email. Again, it's all about testing and experimenting with what works for your market.

Reaching Out

For me, the most reliable outreach has always been via email: "Hello, *company name*. My name is Suzanne Bowness and I've got X years of experience writing narrative long-form blog posts and it seems like you publish those, so why not hire me to write them?" This email is known as a client pitch, prospecting letter, or a client letter of introduction (LOI). Unlike a publication pitch, where your idea is the star, here, you and your experience are the main focus. Ideally your pitch should introduce your services and propose ways that you can help the potential client get their work done more efficiently and cost-effectively. To get in the mindset for sending these pitches, I think of the reasons that I hire outside professionals:

Why would I spend eight times as long trying to figure out my taxes when I could hire my accountant to do it in a quarter of the time and produce a much better result? That's your argument for your own services.

Your letter should also be highly tailored to the industry you're targeting. Pitching to an accounting firm, which may be a highly structured and formal workplace, can be quite different from pitching to a communications agency, which may value creativity and an informal approach.

Here is a sample of a client outreach letter I sent to my current niche: college and university communications departments. In this batch, I reached out to the editors of alumni and research magazines at universities. Note that I focused on my experience and skills that are particularly relevant to that client base and included links to samples that I've written for the same type of client, even though I've written for a wider range of markets. I name drop *University Affairs* magazine, as it is a national publication that would be a prestige market to this audience.

> SUBJECT: Writer/editor introduction
>
> HI X,
>
> I'm a freelance writer and editor interested in connecting about potential story assignments for your alumni magazine, research magazine, or other publications.
>
> I've been freelancing for 20+ years and my portfolio is online at suzannebowness.com. I completed a Ph.D. in English, so I'm familiar with the academic environment, comfortable talking to academics, and interested in promoting university research. I've already worked for several Canadian universities (Carleton University, University of Waterloo, University of Toronto, York University, University of Saskatchewan, Dalhousie University, and others), writing everything from web stories, to research

and alumni magazine articles, to press releases, to editing annual reports.

Here are some samples of my work:

For alumni and research magazines
- *Research Magazine* (Carleton University)
- *York University Magazine* (York University)
- *Hearsay* (Dalhousie University Schulich School of Law)

For Canada's university trade magazine *University Affairs* (universityaffairs.ca)
- Feature on web portfolios [provide link]
- Cover story on students who are also parents [provide link]

Web stories for University of Waterloo
- Building better electric cars
- Student hockey player profile

For more samples, please feel free to visit my portfolio at codeword.ca. Please let me know if you hire freelance writer/editors and how I can keep in touch with you. Also feel free to pass my email along to anyone else in your department who may be looking for writers, as I'm also available for more corporate/marketing work.

Hope you are having a great day and talk to you soon.

Sue

<email signature>

Note that at the end of the letter, I invite the reader to forward the communication to others in their department in order to get more mileage out of the contact. In some LOIs, I get into even more detail about my experience and even reproduce a LinkedIn testimonial. Of course, my email signature contains another link to my contact information and portfolio.

Watch Your Spammer Reputation

A quick word about a wrinkle in the outreach process: the Canadian Anti-Spam Legislation (CASL) — or the equivalent anti-spam law in other countries. Meant to address the real problem of nuisance spammers and their constant offers, the law is unfortunately so broad that it can be interpreted as affecting small businesses. And the fines can be significant.

For me, that means being careful not to follow up too often. Never add someone to your email list without their consent. If they ask you to stop emailing them, stop. If they respond with any touch of a harsh or curt tone, I cut the contact from my list. If you have emailed someone quarterly for two years, maybe try another market. Although it's unlikely that businesses would report an individual looking to provide legitimate services, err on the safe side. It's a judgment call, though sometimes the call made for you by increasingly strong spam filters. When I get tangled in a spam filter (often there's no way to know, but sometimes I receive a bounceback that my email has been rejected) I consider whether it's worth pursing — there are many fish in the potential client sea.

If you don't hear back about a client pitch right away, try not to get discouraged. Much of this success depends on timing and luck. And some of these pitches are long sales cycles — I've had clients not reply to my pitch, then reach out as long as two years later with a lucrative project worth thousands of dollars. Also, the rate of reply to cold pitching is truly low — I've read between 2 and 5 percent? So, for every one hundred emails, you might get two replies — but one might become a client.

Besides these totally cold pitches, you can also try to warm pitch by developing a relationship first: at a networking event or online through a platform like LinkedIn, where you can comment on an editor's post, and they can become familiar with your name over time. If you do meet someone while networking, remember to pitch before they have time to forget who you are, remind the new contact of your connection, and keep up the relationship even if they don't accept your first query. Of course, the warmest is a client you already work for — don't forget to keep in touch regularly and even ask about other opportunities within the organization.

Communications Firms and Agencies

As another option for pitching your services, reach out to communications firms or advertising agencies that already provide editorial services. Rather than working for clients directly, you would work for and be paid by the firm. These agencies can have different focuses, from communications to advertising to public relations, or they can position themselves more generally to offer a range of services.

The advantage is that these agencies already have established client relationships. The disadvantage is that as a subcontractor working in a particular position, either you have no contact with the client (so you have no say in rate negotiation or don't develop a direct relationship), or most agencies will take a cut (sometimes quite substantial) of your rate (although it's work you don't have to find for yourself, which is a huge time savings). For example, Contently is an online service where you can create a portfolio, uploading samples from your niche and advertising yourself as open to corporate work that they arrange through their many clients. You connect with the clients and get paid on their system.

Other agencies might be focused on website development, branding, or advertising, but they often need writers as well. Approach the agencies the same way as approaching the client base, by assembling a list (preferably starting with any that seem to service your niche) and reaching out to them. Generally, the Communications Director, Content Director, or Creative Director will be your targets in terms of titles.

Yet another type of agency is the creative staffing agency, which is similar to general temporary staffing agencies except it serves the creative fields (for example, representing writers, editors, designers, project managers, and others) for short contracts to provide overload editorial support to these companies (or even businesses by sector). Unlike advertising or communications agencies that are pitching to clients to do the work, staffing agencies are pitching to creatives as staff and acting as your agent. If you can get yourself listed as a service provider with one of these companies, it can be a good opportunity to gain work experience (again, the pay is lower to account for their commission).

In both communications firms and staffing agencies, you will probably have to sign non-compete clauses that prevent you from working for the client for a set amount of time after the contract ends. Make sure you're aware of all aspects of the relationship before signing up.

Your Client Mix

Between pitching publications, reaching out both cold and warm to clients, and connecting with agencies, you're eventually going to compile a roster of clients. Yay! While your pitching will be a bit scattershot to start, eventually you'll want to think about the ideal mix of working types and client types. My mix includes at least two or three anchor clients (clients who are regulars and give me enough business that they form a low double-digit percentage of my work and make me feel more secure financially), regular clients who hire me for monthly blog posts or batches of social media posts, and clients who might hire me for one-off projects, like a website, grant application, or a report that will bring in a large sum of money over a short period of time — such projects can be repeat work, but they may be only yearly, as in the case of an annual report.

Ideally you don't want any one client to make up a majority of your income because to lose them can be temporarily disastrous. I've read that it's useful to not have one client make up more than 20 percent of your business, although different people have different thoughts on this limit. At the same time, you want clients who pay well enough that you look forward both to writing for them and paying your rent with the income earned from them. If you've been working for a client regularly for a few projects, you could also broach the subject of a retainer, where they pay a flat fee monthly for a set of services (say, a blog post and X number of social media posts) or for X number of hours or a combination (say, a blog post monthly plus X hours of open time) — this arrangement means that you'll agree to prioritize their requests as a client in return for the client paying you regularly. For example, a recent retainer client paid me for one blog post per month, plus six hours of open time that was used for everything from emails to news releases to social media planning. Ideally you should get retainer clients to sign a contract for a minimum period of time (three to six months is good to start; a year is even better) that specifies the rate and tasks. Another way of trying to attract volume work is by offering a small discount on your rates, say, 10 percent off for more than six blog posts (just make sure the discount is worth your while).

As I mentioned at the outset, your business will be built on serving your clients well, doing excellent work, doing fairly regular outreach to existing clients (repeat business is the best!), and pitching new clients. Over the years, as your business evolves, you may want to try different niches. And you'll definitely want to trade up to higher-paying clients. You may even want to "fire" a client that doesn't treat you well or pays too little. If a client is nice but you've outgrown their pay scale (read: they have a tiny budget), you could consider passing the assignments along to a more junior writer. And even with problem clients, try not to burn any bridges, as your reputation is very important as a freelancer. Equally, don't feel too bad about letting go of a client that isn't serving your business. Because now your business is your first priority!

Chapter 8

Collaborating with Editors and Clients

In a previous chapter, I took you through the journey of writing an article. If you can come up with a half-decent draft, that is the first step toward impressing a client or editor. Having worked both sides of the editorial desk, I can tell when a writer has put a lot of effort into a draft and delivered a product that I can work with. The draft doesn't need to be perfect, and, in fact, I'm much happier with an imperfect draft from an agreeable writer than a better draft written by a diva who is resistant to all my suggestions.

So, I suppose that's the first rule of how to impress an editor. Don't be a diva.

Now, that's not to say, don't stand up for your own work or push back when an editor changes something to make it less accurate because they didn't hear the whole interview so don't have the context you do. It's more to say, keep in mind that an editor's job is twofold: to make your work better and, even more importantly, to stand up for the reader and make sure that they understand everything you wrote. Keeping those elements in mind will help you prioritize collaboration. You're on the same team.

This advice applies equally if you're editing — don't hesitate to explain a change you've made that might be controversial. In fact, an editor gets Editor Points if you not only flag an imprecise word (noted as *word choice*) that "doesn't sound right" but also suggest replacement words (for example, rather than the term "addressing," maybe "counterbalancing" or "offsetting" might be more precise? I'm borrowing an example from a recent edit). Again, we all work better when we share, rather than being writer-divas or editor-keepers-of-the-truth.

I've certainly met editors who push back on silly things, who change words just because they like the word "angry" better than "mad" when it doesn't really make a difference. Side note: if you're in the role of editor, pause before making changes and ask whether the author really got it wrong or if the word is just not your favourite word/style/adjective. If it's wrong, change it. If it's imprecise or unnecessarily complex, flag it (I've changed almost every instance of the word "utilize" to "use" on just about every editing job in the last five years) but otherwise move on. I certainly appreciate editors because they often make me sound better, but I am a better editor because I've been a writer occupying the fragile-ego position of handing in work that I birthed from my brain just to get it back bloodied with red pen (or mostly the modern-day version: Track Changes).

Defining the Assignment

So, what are some ways you can start the editorial relationship off right? In the previous chapter, I mentioned the bonus of having an assignment letter or creative brief and the need to confirm the assignment details if you don't get an assignment letter. Now, just as you don't want the editor to judge you for spelling the word millennial incorrectly because you have a mental block on it (asking for a friend), don't hassle the editor for forgetting or omitting a creative brief. Just send a neutral email and summarize the details. If you do have an assignment letter, try to ask any follow-up questions before you begin; for example, do they want you to interview a particular person or will they ask for a particular form, like a Q&A over a written feature. And here I speak for editing assignments as well. You should be clear on the kind of edit they want — a copy edit with a bit of stylistic editing? A substantive edit? Everything included with fact-checking on top? As I mentioned earlier, sometimes clients don't know exactly what kind of edit they want, so you may need to steer them in a better direction once you've seen the text.

Further intelligence-gathering should happen in a phone call or video conference, which is also great for relationship building. If your editor ever suggests a kick-off call (this will happen more often for bigger projects, say, an annual report, than it will for a one-off blog post), do take it. Before you have this meeting, look over the organization's website, including its About page, organizational chart, or staff listing if available (if only to ascertain where your supervisor sits within the organization), and browse their social platforms. Search the organization and your contact online to see what links come up first, and you can even look up your supervisor on LinkedIn, unless that seems too awkward. Look for any existing samples of the form you've been tasked to create, try to discern the audience and tone, and make notes on anything you might need to ask for if it isn't online.

Your presence on the call should be mostly as a listener, trying to grasp the project parameters within the set time frame of the call (shorter is better; you have made a new contact, not a new friend, so chit-chat to start, but get down to business when they signal to do so). If they ask if you have any questions for them, do ask any questions that are outstanding. But while you should confirm your fee and payment timeline, try to avoid too many questions that focus only on your own self-interest. If you understand the project, a nice question is one that shows your interest in the organization, such as how the communications department operates. For instance, how many people are on the communications team and who handles what?

The Editorial Dance

As you get started on the project, further questions may come up that you may not have been able to anticipate in the kick-off call. Again, look on the organization's website (or in the style guide) first for answers. If you don't find the answers, do not hesitate to reach back out, especially if those answers will stop you from going off in a wrong direction. I recently made an editorial decision while copy editing a document to change all instances of a particular word, only to have to change it back later. I should have sent an email. If you end up with several questions and the answers won't stop you from moving forward, consider bundling your questions in one email so you're not asking a question per day. Keep your editor's busy workflow in mind and the fact that yours is likely not their only project.

In terms of keeping in touch with your editor through the project, that need depends on the size of the assignment, your editor's own rhythm, and your progress. Some editors are fine not to hear back from you until deadline day, while others appreciate weekly check-ins. If an editor asks for these check-ins, then you have your answer. If they say nothing, I still like to check in periodically on a larger project, especially if I've passed a milestone in the project that they may wonder about, such as securing all the interviews. If the editor mentioned that it might be hard to reach interviewees for a feature article, I might reach out once I've scheduled the interviews to reassure the editor that everything is on track. If it's a straightforward blog post, feel free to just make your next contact the submission.

Another reason to check in is if the assignment is going in a different (read: bad) direction. Maybe you pitched an article idea thinking you'd find a bunch of people who were willing to share their experiences with a certain toe fungus, and it turns out everyone's too shy to chat about it, so you need to pivot to relying mostly on expert doctors quoting their patients anonymously. Maybe it turns out the toe fungus is easily cured with a topical ointment and it's really no big deal; i.e., there's not really a story where you thought there would be. The sooner you can have a conversation with your editor about how to handle a new direction, the better you'll be able to stay on track with your deadline. The editing equivalent might be to realize that a document really needs a structural and/or line edit rather than the copy edit that the client requested — the end result will be a better product, but the client might be shocked (both by the number of changes and the higher invoice reflecting the extra work) if you don't give them a heads-up.

To handle this conversation professionally, think about how you'll summarize the issue and come up with a couple of solutions on your own (a list of expert doctors to call on about the toe fungus, for example). Sometimes these clarifications can be handled via a short email chain, while longer projects may need a phone call, in which case use email to establish the problem, then ask your editor's advice. While you want to be prepared with solutions, ultimately this is also a time to listen to your client/editor's suggestions, as they may have more experience dealing with these situations and, after all, it's their organization.

A time when it's not great, but necessary, to check in is if you've procrastinated on an assignment and you're behind for no good reason. No, don't risk your mental health if you're gnashing teeth and weeping at your keyboard — your editor will probably be fine if you send in your assignment after a weekend rather than before it. But beyond factors outside your control (an interviewee was on vacation so you couldn't connect with them until yesterday; the news conference you were covering was bumped to next week), you should try to stick to your deadline.

When I've been a slouch, I either stay up late to finish the piece and meet my deadline or, if I foresee that I'll miss it, I let my editor know as soon as possible and come up with my own plan for submission that fits their deadline as closely as possible (a Monday instead of Friday, for example, or an end-of-day at midnight rather than 5:00 p.m.). Being on time is especially important when you are building a new relationship with an editor or client.

Being Patient

So, you've navigated an assignment, submitted your best first draft on deadline, and then ... You. Wait. If it's an assignment with a tight timeline that needs to go out right away, you'll likely hear back in a timely fashion. But if it's something non-urgent, just another part of the editor's workflow, it's likely you'll have to wait a few days — during which certain questions are bound to crop up, especially if you're a new writer, but they are surprisingly persistent even for a long-time writer. Questions like, I haven't heard back from them, what if they hate my draft and are just figuring out how to tell me in a way that doesn't hurt my feelings? What if they are taking this time to hire a completely different writer to salvage the story, one who will also get the fee that they promised to me? (You should get most of it: see the discussion about kill fees in the chapter on pricing.) If you're an editor, this self-doubt can still plague you: What if I didn't catch absolutely everything (rest assured, you probably didn't — but you likely made the document a lot better). If you're working for a corporate or government client, the article may be moving through a glacial, multi-departmental editing and approvals process that you will want to avoid being part of anyway.

Beware this negative self-talk. Replace it with a reminder of what is more likely the case: the editor is busy. They have five other articles to read besides yours. Those other articles are really terrible, and they are taking the time to write thoughtful, sensitive fix notes to the poor hacks that submitted them. Trust that the work will come back when it's ready. After all, you're a confident professional whose self-worth doesn't depend on a single article. Plus, your dog needs an extra walk today and more attention than usual. And you probably have two or three more assignments that need starting. Or a new pitch to write up for that new magazine you picked up the other week. So, who has time to obsessively check their inbox every hour for a response? Not you, that's for sure.

Navigating Feedback

You will likely get an average editor who will supply a standard amount of feedback, some of which you agree with and some of which you think is nit-picky. Brace yourself when you open your document. Most editors today work with Microsoft Word's Track Changes or Google Docs suggestion features, where they can add a combination of comments and direct strikethroughs or additions to your text, plus notes in comments. First, try to just scan the notes and assess the changes required. Sometimes you're lucky and there are few to no changes. Hooray! Don't overthink and wonder if the editor didn't really read it; just accept the compliment of few changes.

After your peek, regardless of which way it went, close your document and put it away for a couple of hours. If it's a bigger fix, you'll likely have a few days to work on it (a week has been pretty standard for me for longer features, say, over 1,000 words). Then approach the revision from large to small. Did the editor ask you to incorporate other interviews or research? That will take the longest time, so approach that outreach right away. No point in working on sentences when new paragraphs are going to be inserted.

Most good editors know to word their comments diplomatically and politely. (Editors take note that this diplomacy wins Editor Points as well and is likely to get the writer on your side.) But the comments still represent a work list. Start with suggestions that push you to change the text more substantively — for example, to expand on a point, add a statistic, or revise a confusing section. If you look at the section and find it perfectly clear — what was the editor thinking? — try to put yourself on their side of the computer screen and think about how else it could be interpreted. If you really cannot figure out how to fix it, reply to their comment, asking for clarification on their clarification (this back and forth can get very meta).

Revising

Slowly work your way through the comments that ask you to add new material or significantly change the text, then on to stuff that is more straightforward — awkward wordings, URLs that don't work, and finally, accept or reject the editor's strikethroughs and additions. If you have queries of your own, or if some comments the editor made clearly stem from their not understanding your greater knowledge of the story, then add a comment in reply to clarify your meaning and see if they still want the change.

While feedback, particularly on a written piece, will mostly happen in this civilized forum of Track Changes, where editors politely sidestep the tone-deafness of email, and writers grit their teeth as they respond (do grit your teeth, even feel free to swear under your breath at an editor; first, it can be really therapeutic, and also, how will they know?), sometimes your editor or client will ask to discuss your draft over the phone or video conference, particularly with a longer story or project.

First, don't read too much into the meeting; likely they'll have a set of prepared notes to help you see where the project has gone wrong, and you'll have to gain control over your teeth gritting to get through it. Because there is a correct response to this feedback: thank you.

I smile when I think about this answer because one's first inclination when hearing feedback is to explain why you did it your (wrong) way. This only comes across as defensive and underconfident. When I was teaching a project management course to my writing students who were presenting a marketing plan to a live client, I had the students pitch the idea to me first, and then I gave them feedback. Of course, they started to explain themselves, which I cut off and countered with the idea of the "thank you." Before long, as team after team couldn't resist breaking in with their reasons, we were all giggling at the fact that it's so hard to just sit with the feedback. Through the term, "thank you" became a trigger for shared glances and quick lip purses as we practised being gracious. By the time we met with the client, they were the most professional and polished group of students.

After you've handled your first revision and sent it back to the editor, you may have another round of touch-ups: the editor will respond to your queries, maybe ask a few more, or have another colleague read it, which could prompt more questions. At each stage, reread it yourself, tightening sentences and looking for errors. Depending on the size of the magazine or organization, they may also do a separate copy edit using a style guide to ensure consistency (Do they use honorifics like Ms. or Mr.? Do they use periods in country abbreviations, e.g., U.S. vs US? Is the organization's preferred spelling "policy makers" or "policy-makers?")

If you are an editor, unless you're part of a team where there will be many rounds of editing, submission may be where the cycle ends. It does for me and many of my corporate editing clients who tend to want just a smart pair of eyes on something to bring it in line with the style guide, copy edit it, and fix the footnotes. You send in your edit, your client thanks you, and ... silence. You wonder, *Did I do a good job?* While you can ask for feedback from a client, it's not generally part of the process. You assume you did a good job when you are asked to take on another assignment.

Fact-Checking

Another editing practice that is unfortunately falling out of habit in newspaper and magazine publishing is fact-checking — only the biggest, wealthiest magazines now invest in this essential service, and even some of these publications are dropping the practice. So, make time to conduct your own fact-check — at minimum double-check name spellings and titles, places, and quotes (that damned AI transcription can fool us all!). If you are lucky enough as a writer to get an outside fact-checker, make it easy for them by providing all of your interviewee contacts and any research materials. Of course, occasionally false facts get through (I always remember the time I turned a CEO from a Tim into a Tom in a national newspaper), but these checks add little time to your process.

All of these efforts are in aid of making your piece the cleanest, most readable, and engaging it can be. After all, both you and your editor(s) share the common goal of a better piece — not a perfect piece, because those don't exist, and you'll stress yourself out if you try to go there.

If you're a freelance editor, you might consider building fact-checking into your workflow, either unofficially or more formally. I often include a "complimentary online fact-check" in my quotes for editing projects, which means that I will google any location names or association acronyms or other easily verified information. These checks result in so many wins, it's a very low-effort way of impressing a client, and when you can find those wins, treat them like gold.

Approvals Process

A final stage in the editing process can sometimes be an approvals process. For organizations, often the approvals happen through a hierarchy; for example, a junior editor will share with a senior editor, or a communications specialist will share with their director. Approvals processes often depend on how large or bureaucratic the organization is — for example, government approvals can be very lengthy. The extent of approvals can also depend on how important the text is. For example, many people may want to weigh in on a website revision that will stay online and represent the organization for a few years versus a blog post or social media posting (although I've heard about an approvals process for social media posts in government). Most often, these approvals are handled internally, although the writer could be asked for fixes again. Ideally try to have one point of contact within the organization (hopefully the editor who originally assigned you) and know who has final say on the text (in case of competing feedback).

Another approval level can be with interviewees, and today's writer is asked to get involved more often than they used to, mainly because they are already the point of contact and have a relationship via the interview. This is where journalistic writing for organizations differs from actual journalism. If you're writing for a journalistic publication, it is very much against practice to show quotes to an interviewee. Interviewees often WILL ask about approvals though, at which point you can tell them it's not the usual, but you'll let your editor know they're interested (I love playing good cop/bad cop with editors and often invite my editors to feel free to blame things on the silly writer). If interviewees do get upset, truly do put them in touch with your editor, who can explain journalistic principles.

If you're working for an organization where the piece is journalistic (quotes from interviews that are woven together and read like a story that would be published in the media) but is more or less positive press used as a marketing tool, then it's customary to show your quotes to the interviewee. This happens a lot with my university clients, for example, where the client wants the researcher to see the piece before it is posted online so they can be sure I've captured their work correctly. This can happen in a few ways, from sharing the whole piece, to sharing just their quotes with each interviewee, to sharing just their sections with each interviewee. Ask your editor what they prefer before sharing the quotes. If you've written a fair piece and captured what the interviewee says, they'll most often sign off on it with few changes and maybe even compliment you on capturing their story. I get this response a lot — it's a nice feeling.

Of course, there will always be the occasional interviewee who will respond like a bad editor and want to change every word. Often, they'll change wording or trim the fun anecdotes to sound more in line with the key messages of the company, but the changes make the quotes sound stilted and lifeless. You may be able to push back on this approach (tell interviewees that the article and sharing of stories make them sound relatable and human), or, again, feel free to get your editor involved.

I have mixed feelings about the approvals process. On the one hand, I'm relieved to have my smart physicist professor interviewee who originated the facts look them over as a second check on my arts-major capture. On the other hand, it adds another layer to the process, and when you get a fuss-pot, it can make the story a bit worse. Several years ago, internal teams managed this process and writers were rarely asked to handle approvals; today, it's much more common. Of course, this extra work adds time to your workload, which you're expected to absorb. Today, writers are even requested to ask after photos — often editors will want everything from a headshot of each interviewee to action shots to accompany your article — at a high resolution suitable for print. This expectation irks me, as it's even further removed from writing. But again, as an agreeable writer who is a Team Player, I generally say this extra ask is fine, except when I'm asked to do so much that I begin feeling like a doormat, at which point I push back a tiny bit, and usually receive an apology rather than an offer to take the work back.

To recap: the route to impressing an editor is do what you say you were going to do, submit when you said you would, accept feedback with grace, be generally easy to work with, and think about ways you can make their lives easier. All this effort will ideally be reciprocated with gratitude, an editor that is also easy to work with, and the holy grail of freelancing: a repeat client.

Score One for the Freelancer: Repeat Business

Once you've entered this very happy place called repeat business, treasure these relationships like gold. Given how difficult it can be to land a client, finding one that comes to you with more work can be very lucrative. The way to stay in that happy place is to continue to produce excellent work that meets and exceeds the standard you set with the first project, plus keep in touch on a regular basis. More on ways to augment your reputation in the chapter on branding and networking.

THE FEISTY FREELANCER

© Iva Cheung

Chapter 9

Productivity 101

The best thing about working for yourself is that you have no boss. The worst thing about working for yourself is that you have no boss.

No boss means nobody to organize your time, prioritize your tasks, or make you feel guilty about how little you've accomplished in an hour, a day, a month (although you'll get good at making your own guilt trips). So, you have to develop tactics for organizing yourself and your time. Or you can just read this chapter, where I'm going to share some techniques that have worked for me that will hopefully provide a shortcut for you. Remember that different tactics work for different people, so try a few and adopt what works.

As I mentioned earlier, I think it's easiest to work when others are working. For those in North America, this timing often means a 9:00 a.m. to 5:00 p.m. schedule, or 8:00 to 4:00, or 7:00 to 3:00, whatever works for you. I know many busy parent freelancers who work after the kids have left for school and stop when it's time to pick them up. For those who work on the North American west coast serving east coast clients, it might mean starting early in Vancouver to meet the business day in New York.

Whatever hours you choose to work, try making a regular schedule or find a balance between the hours you'd like to work and what you think fits best for your clients. Because I hate to say it, but I do see some correlation between income and butt-in-seat time. Yes, a freelancer's schedule is flexible, but you do need to do the work. So, figure out a time frame that works for you.

Creating Your Schedule

Within your day, you might also identify your most productive times. Try to do your deep work then. For writers, that's usually writing or structuring stories, creating pitches, working on edits, or other thought-requiring tasks. For editors, it can be tackling a first pass through a document. I schedule routine tasks like invoicing and other administrative tasks for my sleepy first hour of the morning while I sip my tea, unless someone has called me into a meeting. I used to check email for that first hour of the morning but found myself sliding into a full hour for email and social checks, which is too much. Now I am trying this different approach. See? Productivity is a skill that you can work on.

I schedule business planning for Friday afternoons, when my deadlines are usually done for the week and I feel a little freer. If I am working on projects requiring calls and interviews, I try to schedule interviews at least an hour apart in case they go long, and I try not to schedule more than three interviews or client calls a day, or else I feel really exhausted. Of course, this preference goes out the window if it's convenient for a hard-to-book client to schedule at a particular time of day. The client is queen.

I block my schedule into periods of a couple of hours so I'm not constantly task switching. For example, I save up all my invoices for the week and do them in the same two hours — same thing with pitches, writing social posts, and writing assignments. It's a personalized, feel-it-out thing, but I need a couple of hours to get into a task like copy editing a report, then I need a break from editing, and then from something else like an administrative task. I reply to email and direct messages on my social platforms and voicemails just two or three times per day and shut down my email program when I'm doing focused work.

I try to stretch (or go into the kitchen to make a fresh tea; or into the living room to pat a cat) about every hour or so. I use television as a longer break, generally taking twenty minutes in the morning, another twenty minutes in the afternoon, as well as a half-hour for lunch. I almost never eat at my desk because I find the break away refreshing, especially when I fill the break with something other than looking at my computer screen. Whether television or a phone call or a walk outside, I choose an activity that provides the head clearing I need to be fresh. By head clearing, I mean a complete distraction rather than just moving to another location to continue thinking about the assignment I've been obsessing about. I find this especially with editing — if I keep editing beyond my optimal time, my powers of concentration go right down and I end up reading the same paragraph over and over, so what is the point? When you can, take a few minutes to relax and refresh.

As I mentioned, I try to end my day around 5:00 p.m., and if I need to work late because I'm behind on a project, then I take a break at that time and return to work rather than just sliding into the evening.

Dealing with Writer's Block

Yes, it's a thing. Yes, we all get it. But for professional writers who make words their living, I notice writer's block is a thing that happens a lot less often. Paying the rent is a powerful motivator.

When you have writer's block, and your living depends on writing, you get good at figuring out how to get out of the block. The worst thing you can do is stare at a blank page. So, what else can you do? My favourite tactics include brainstorming around the topic, writing an outline of the piece, starting in the middle of the piece to write the easiest part of it (as opposed to the opening, where writer's block only worsens), or reading some background about your topic (CAREFUL not to let this background research turn into an internet rabbit hole).

If none of these strategies works, you may permit yourself to take a SHORT walk/shower/laundry break/cat playtime break/refrigerator cleanup session/bookshelf rearrangement session — something that occupies your body while leaving your mind relatively free to ponder the problem. No TV at this writing moment, as it will just distract you. Ditto a social media break. As soon as your mind wanders to pick away at the problem, follow it there. Ideally the ideas will start to flow, and you can get back to either writing a section of the piece you had the idea for, or adding to the outline, or researching something that will prompt more writing. Write one paragraph on the easiest part of the article, then write another one. Or look for a quote that you know you'll incorporate and try to build around it.

If you're absolutely stuck and you have the time before deadline (this is why it helps to start projects as soon as possible, so that you can plan for blocks), try working on another task you're feeling less blocked about and return to the troublesome assignment in the afternoon or the next morning. Just be careful to keep on it, because this unwritten assignment is a monster that grows in your mind the more you leave it be.

Speaking of monsters, a lot of my students mention that perfectionism is another mindset issue that can really get in the way. I challenge students on this hurdle by suggesting they submit an assignment when they think it is at 90 percent of their best rather than 100 percent and see how much time (and stress!) they save. Again, I think being a working writer scares away the perfectionism because you wouldn't succeed if you couldn't meet your deadline, but when you're getting started, you need to train yourself to let go. If it helps, think of an uncomfortable submission as making room for the editor to contribute their part to your piece. Writing might be solo, but it's rarely without collaboration.

Other Time Tricks: Pomodoros and Batching

Now that you've dealt with the time-waster that is writer's block and the mindset crusher that is perfectionism, let's turn to other tactics that will help you get the most out of your writerly day. Pomodoro is a much-shared technique ("pomodoro" is the Italian word for tomato; the technique is named for a tomato-shaped kitchen timer that originator Francesco Cirillo used) that suggests that you work for a period of time, then take a short break. By limiting your time, you focus your efforts and feel like you can be off the clock at a predictable time.

Trick's on you, though, because often by the time you've exhausted the official pomodoro time, you're well into the groove and don't feel like you need the break as much. I use a nice thirty-minute hourglass with ten minute breaks in between and deploy these sprints, especially when I'm having a hard time getting started with a story, when I need to edit down an interview, or when I need to keep focused for an end-of-day deadline.

Another time-saving tactic that helps me is batching tasks. I already mentioned that I handle invoicing within the same two hours and answer emails twice a day rather than as they come in. But batching also works for tasks I want to accomplish in my own business, such as creating my newsletter or writing LinkedIn posts. Rather than write my posts one at a time the day before they're scheduled, I try to write four weekly posts in the same afternoon once a month, or sometimes even once a quarter. That little week between Christmas and New Year that I love (Q5!) is a great time for some of this content production. The posts don't have to be perfected during the batch, but everyone knows that the first draft is the hardest, so it's a real break if you can knock out a few at a time, and all you have to do later is edit. Plus, it's another task-switching save: once you get into the groove of writing the posts, it's easier to keep going.

Some also refer to this focused time as "time blocking," whereby you're not task switching so much that you have to refocus every half-hour on something new. Put alike tasks together if you can. Also, multitasking? Not a thing.

Productivity can also come from tools. I use a social media scheduler to load posts in advance and schedule blog posts into my website. I mentioned my experiment with a calendar-sharing feature that allows others to schedule their own interviews with me (be careful here to integrate the app with your desktop calendar so that you're not double-booking — I learned this goof the hard way at the start), which saves some back and forth. I use a project management tool to list all of my projects and what stage they are at. A bookkeeping app reminds me about which invoices I need to follow up on.

Hiring an Assistant

One of my best investments has been to hire a virtual assistant to help with some basic tasks in order to free up my time for work that moves my business forward. I dislike social media, but I know that building my authority through sharing information is important, so I task the assistant with scanning twenty-five or so websites that I used to visit myself on a weekly basis and coming up with a batch of links that I can choose from. Then the assistant drafts the posts and puts them into my scheduler. I'm also getting them to create first drafts of my invoices and research possible new client niches. A productivity aside: I almost never pitch to clients by composing a fresh email but, rather, use templates that I personalize like a templated letter of introduction; I also have templates for standard interview requests and editor follow-ups. I've already shared the LOI and the interview request templates with you in previous chapters; feel free to modify and adapt them for your own use. You're welcome.

Now, the scary element of hiring an assistant is that you need to hand off work that you once did and secretly believe only you can do, from social media posts to invoice creation. At first, it feels like the handover is so much work that you might as well continue to do it yourself. Resist this thought pattern. Once you get the task shifted, you will recover the time. Another hesitation can be the fear of handing over something integral to your business. Again, build in some protections if you are feeling hesitant. For example, I have my assistant find links to share on my socials, but I still make the final selection and approve posts in the scheduler. I still hit send on my own invoices, even if the assistant creates them.

Besides an assistant, I also look for other areas where I can create shortcuts or give myself time, even if it's just for more rest. I regularly order takeout every week or two to give myself a break from meal prep. The dishwasher is my favourite appliance, I no longer buy clothing that requires hand washing. I hire someone to mow my lawn and shovel snow from my driveway.

The point is that self-employment (and life in general) can be hard enough, so it's great to look for shortcuts, especially if they allow you to work on your business.

Yet another way to think of increasing productivity is to increase your rates. If you make more money, you work less to make the same income, and it's almost like getting time. Are there ways that you can charge more for your services or add services without adding much time (I regularly upsell clients on social posts to boost an article; it's easy enough to create an extra Instagram or Facebook post when I'm immersed in the article topic already, and it's something of value to them). Can you take on clients in a niche that pays more money than your current niche? This productivity-oriented thinking can be key to freeing up even more time.

Coda: Relaxation 101

Burnout is real.

Planning time away from your desk, whether it be in the evenings, weekends, or for vacation, is essential to maintaining the stamina required for creative work. Time with your family, visits with friends, space for hobbies, and true vacations can all help you stay in love with your lovely freelance life. Set downtime goals and parameters for yourself. Mine include not working on weekends unless absolutely necessary, quitting at 5:00 p.m., and only returning to work if on a deadline (and not making late nights a habit). I am grateful to be able to take at least a three-week travel holiday most years in the summer, plus a week-long winter break around February (because Canadian winters suck).

On a daily level, plan in breaks as well. If you've worked late to meet a deadline, allow yourself to sleep in for an hour. If you have a dentist appointment, feel free to add on an hour to run errands or go shopping rather than going right back to your desk. Now, if you did this add-on with every appointment, every day, then it might violate the butt-in-seat rule that helps to keep the business going, but the point is to take advantage of the lifestyle perks you set up for yourself by choosing freelancing.

As we become more aware of mental health issues, check in with yours periodically. If you're doing work that you have control over, that practice should improve your mental health, not worsen it. If you feel overworked or you're starting to burn out, try to take action before it becomes a real drag on your work or life. Take a long weekend. If you've been working late every night one week, look for ways to get back in balance. Maybe it means getting help by subcontracting or outsourcing your work to a colleague. Or maybe your family life is becoming really busy — is there something you could do there to provide some relief? Maybe you need to cut back on work hours for a period of time. Maybe you need to break your vow temporarily to avoid weekend work, in order to feel less stressed (hello from my desk on Sunday at 2:00 p.m., editing this book). If you have a major crisis, consider taking a short leave. When my father passed away, I called all my editors and just gave up my stories or lined up a freelance friend to take over, knowing that I wouldn't be in any frame of mind to work for a few weeks. People were really understanding, and they will be with you too. Experiment with what works, and don't just settle for being chronically, low-grade unhappy.

All of these balancing efforts keep me whole and human and help to maintain the feisty.

© Iva Cheung

Chapter 10

Pricing Services, Getting Paid

Finally, we arrive at pricing — one of my favourite subjects simply because I believe knowledge is power, and if we share pricing information as freelancers we can all increase the chances of being paid what we're worth. Unlike some industries with licencing or unions to regulate their pricing, writing/editing can be a bit of a wild west, with the prices varying wildly. In fact, I got so invested in the idea of reporting beyond my own pricing strategies that I created my informal freelancer survey primarily to get a sense of the range of rates people charge. It only confirmed that there is no consistent answer.

Pricing Approaches

Let's start with approaches to pricing. One way is to keep track of your time and bill by the hour. Different freelancers price services in different ways: some charge one fee for all services, some charge different fees for different services.

I charge somewhat less for editing and proofreading than I do for writing. I also have a price range (not huge) rather than a fixed price for all clients. For example, I might charge less for a small non-profit than for a large institutional corporate client. But not much less. I try not to make assumptions that just because a business is a non-profit means it doesn't have a budget.

By contrast, some writers charge one rate for all tasks. To the question in my informal survey "Do you charge the same price or different prices for different services?" 27 percent charged the same price for different services and 73 percent of respondents charged different prices. Before I start any project, I try to find out the client's or publication's budget so I can get a sense of what is considered standard in this particular market. I've found most clients are reluctant to share budgets. If a client's rate is too low, I ask the client if they can do better and sometimes have to let them down gently if they don't have the budget. Maybe a junior writer who charges less is more within their budget?

To figure out what hourly rate to charge, try talking to other freelancers in your industry niche and see what their rates are. You might also talk to potential clients and see if they have a standard rate of pay. Among my gang of anonymous freelance writer/editor respondents, forty-eight of the sixty respondents gave their rates to my question, "What is your hourly rate for writing services?"

The informal data on page 145 reflects a few elements that I've heard anecdotally: that most writer/editors are charging above $50 hourly, but few are making above $125; the majority charge between $70 and $125 per hour for writing services. And that there is a pretty wide range out there, and that possibly we should be comparing wages more regularly to ensure that we are making what we are worth. Also, newer editors may want to start at a lower rate as they build experience, say, in the $40 to $50 range. Likely, the higher rates above reflect longer experience, but they can also reflect the confidence to experiment with pricing and charge more. After all, freelancers need to factor their expenses, overhead, missing benefits, and administration time into their pricing.

What is your hourly rate for writing services?

Hourly rate range ($/hr)	No. of respondents (%)* (n = 48)
30–40	4.2
40–50	8.3
50–60	12.5
60–70	10.4
70–80	8.3
80–90	6.3
90–100	18.8
100–125	20.8
125–150	6.3
125–200	4.2

*Rounded

On the upside, nobody reported asking below $30 hourly despite my answer categories including "under $25 hourly."

Editing rates started as low as $25 per hour and ranged as high as $125 per hour among the survey respondents who answered my question, "What is your hourly rate for editing services?" (see page 146).

The majority of respondents are charging between $60 and $100 hourly. These hourly rates reflect what I've heard anecdotally from editors, and also the fact that, again, there is a wide range, which makes me hope that anyone whose rates are on the lower end will consider raising them when they learn what others charge. Some of the respondents may be newer editors, but some may well not be charging enough. Newcomers to the industry have the challenge of trying to set prices that reflect their lower experience level but are not so low that they can't pay their bills. As I tell my students, you didn't work hard at developing these skills just to charge minimum wage.

What is your hourly rate for editing services?

Hourly rate range ($/hr)	No. of respondents (%)* (n = 46)
25–30	4.3
30–40	4.3
40–50	8.7
50–60	10.8
60–70	23.9
70–80	17.3
80–90	8.7
90–100	17.9
100–125	2.1

*Rounded

Another long-standing, if odd, payment tradition in journalism and editorial circles is to charge by the word. For example, national newspapers generally pay around $0.50 per word, so for an 800 to 1,000-word story you'd be paid $500. The top paying national magazines in Canada pay $1 per word (sometimes up to $1.25 or even $1.50 or higher for an experienced freelancer). Smaller magazines and trade publications might pay around $0.40 to $0.70 a word. When I asked my anonymous freelancers, "What is your most common per-word rate for writing?" the most common answers were $1.00 to $1.25 per word (over 33 percent) and $0.90

per word (almost 27 percent). Around 17 percent reported getting $0.40 to $0.60 per word. I usually aim for $1.00 a word and try not to write for less than $0.50 per word.

In the United States, not only is the word rate higher but the dollar is worth more than in Canada, which is why we're more likely to try to break into your market than you are into ours, American friends. I recall meeting some freelancers at an event in New York and receiving some pitying looks when telling my new friends that I worked mostly for magazines in Canada. The bigger magazines in the U.S. pay as much as $3 or more per word, which is sort of like hearing that jars of peanut butter cost $30. What?

Other useful places to go for a pricing check are the occasional regular surveys published by writing and editing groups. Here are a few examples; note that these are American outfits, so prices are all in U.S. dollars. The American Writers and Artists Institute (AWAI; see awai.com) is a provider of copywriting training programs. The annual Copywriting Pricing Guide lists dozens of forms (mostly copywriting) and the averages that writers charge. In the 2024 edition, for example, the report listed $250–$800 as the range for blog posts of 300–1,000 word, and $1,200–$2,000 as the range for case studies (a corporate format that involves writing a journalistic-style writeup to tell a customer solution story). For copy editing, the average rate was $31–$75 an hour, or $0.03 to $0.05 a word. The Copywriter Club, whose focus is similarly on copywriting, published an Income Report in 2021 in which they surveyed five hundred copywriters. Results were broken down by years of copywriting experience; the average fee charged by copywriters with one to two years of experience for blog posts was $361 (median $250), and for case studies the average was $712 (median $325). Copywriters with five to ten years of experience charged $498 per blog post (median $300) and $1,557 (median $650) for case studies, and copywriters with ten-plus years of experience charged an average of $482 (median $314) for blog posts and $1,094 for case studies (median $675). To view the survey in full, visit thecopywriterclub.com/how-much-copywriters-paid. The Editorial Freelancers Association (EFA; see the-efa.org) publishes a rate card that lists pricing per hour, per word, and per page. It breaks down copy editing into niches from academic to technical, with rates ranging from $40 to $65 hourly. Developmental and line editing services range from $45 to $70 hourly, and proofreading from $35 to $65 hourly.

Of course, with the increase in types of writing opportunities brought on by this era of internet and social media (websites and blogs and social posts, oh my!), the market has become even wilder. At one point, websites and blogs were trying to get writers to work for much less than a livable wage compared to writing for print. As organizations started to realize the value of web content and blogs, this unpredictability has been mitigated somewhat, although there is still a range. As a newcomer magazine writer, you will be asked to write for "exposure," and the publication will try to woo you with a picture of their huge readership numbers hanging on your every word. Try not to be drawn in. Yes, you need to gain writing samples (also known in the industry as "clips") and experience, but I would seriously avoid outfits that offer as low as $25 or even $50 for a 300-word blog post.

If you do need to write for free to get some clips, make sure it is for a reputable outlet and that you limit the work either to a pre-determined number of clips or to a time frame, say, three to four months. Then trade up as soon as possible to better gigs. For a freelancer starting out, try not to work for less than $0.30 per word, or $25 to $40 per hour. I plead with my fellow senior freelancers not to work for $0.10 or $0.20 a word just because a magazine may have prestige.

Contemplating Your Worth

Even if a gig is proposed to you on a per-word basis, the best way to figure out whether to take the gig is to calculate whether it meets your hourly rate. Think about how long it will take to write the stories (factor in research, interviews and transcribing, writing, revisions, emailing back and forth) and see if the per-word rate gives you a decent hourly rate. If it doesn't, consider asking for more money or turning down the story. Or you might decide that a lower rate is worth the investment if the gig will give you other intangible benefits (a publication credit in a national newspaper if you have none, for example).

However, do not kid yourself that writing a 200-word blog post for $20 will be okay because you can do it in thirty minutes and thus make $40 per hour. Yes, that strategy might work to begin with, but that pace of work is not sustainable. Furthermore, accepting and, therefore, validating such low pay rates is the scourge of our industry. This harms all freelancers. Yes, I realize I'm speaking from a point of privilege, being already established with writing samples and contacts, but as soon as you can charge reasonable rates, trade up.

When calculating the feasibility of client projects, another approach is to propose a flat fee rather than an hourly rate. Often, this approach helps a client to understand the entire fee and whether or not it fits into their budget. Calculate this fee based not only on your hourly rate but also on how much value it brings to the client. This approach is also a way to account for the speed of senior-level freelancers, who may work much faster than junior writers and therefore may make less for a similar workload if charging an hourly rate.

You should also try to give yourself a raise periodically. You can accomplish this in a few ways. If you have been working for a publication for a couple of years and they keep hiring you because they like your work, why not ask for an extra $0.10 a word? And if they say no, keep asking, say, every six months. Try at times that seem like natural change points — for example, when a new editor comes on board (or maybe after the first story you write for the client that has shown off your amazing style). Or the New Year can be a good time. If you're pitching projects and basing your estimates on an hourly rate, try raising your rate by $2 or $5 and see what happens. Or try raising your hourly rate when someone asks you for it directly. Manitoba-based writer Susan Peters asks for a cost-of-living raise each year from a long-time regular client. The point is, we deserve raises but we won't get them until we ask.

Estimating

Before starting a project, clients will often ask you to provide an estimate or quote. This is more the case when you're pitching a more complex project, such as a report, but even a client who is asking for a blog post wants to know your rate. Journalistic publications will often have an established word rate, so once you've asked, then you decide whether that works for you (or talk it up; sometimes you can get an extra $0.10, especially when you can insist you have the writing experience or lived experience as a source). Even experienced freelancers can find estimating a challenge. The client's goal is to find the most cost-effective writer, but one who also has the skills to handle their project with professionalism. So, it's not always the least expensive writer who will get the work, although many clients are very price conscious. Depending on the project size, firms will often source quotes from two or three freelancers before deciding who to assign the work to.

In creating a quote, try to figure out how much time you think the project will take to complete and multiply those hours by your hourly rate. Where possible, you should ask for the client's budget, although most will dodge providing a hard number.

If possible, ask to see a sample of the project, particularly if it is an editing project. If you ask for a five-page sample of the work, time yourself working on a couple of pages to see how long each one takes to edit, then figure out a total number of hours based on the length of the manuscript. If the document is thirty pages long, and one page takes you twenty minutes to copy edit, it will take you ten hours to complete the project.

You should account for any meetings, administrative back and forth (phone calls, emails), background research, interviewing time, outlining time, drafts (first, second), and time for revisions (factor in at least two passes). And add a bit of a buffer (10–20 percent is fairly standard) in case the rest of the pages turn out to be much worse than the sample they sent, or the client changes their mind about what they want. Note the limitations of your estimate within your quote — for example, how many revisions are included (two is fairly standard for writing projects), and what to do if the project turns out to be a lot longer than you expected (typically that you'll either revisit the quote or charge your hourly rate for any overtime). If you're asked to do the project quickly or at an inconvenient time, like over a weekend, some writers charge a rush fee on top of their quote, starting around 15 percent and up to as much as 50 percent or higher.

The good news about estimating is that it does get easier with experience, particularly if you end up taking on similar projects where you know how much time they will take. Track your time and start keeping a record so that you get to know your speed for various assignments. Some freelancers even go so far as to develop a "rate card" that spells out how much they charge for standard projects — for example, $500 for a media release or $4,500 for a white paper. When I asked my anonymous freelancers what they charge as a flat rate for blog posts, 42 percent said they charge their hourly rate, 13 percent are charging $400–$500, and 10 percent charge $300–$400 and $200–$300, respectively.

The downside of estimating is that even if you get better at this challenging skill, a project can take longer than you think, and you have to decide whether to absorb the extra hours or ask for more money, which might annoy the client. If a project goes way "out of scope" you would be justified in having a conversation about billing more hours than originally anticipated, and you should try to speak as soon as you can with your supervisor on the project.

Contracts

After your quote has been accepted (congratulations!), put a contract in place to solidify terms of the project. Some workplaces are less formal and don't use contracts, although good contracts are helpful for your mutual protection. If a client does not offer a contract, you can draw one up yourself. You don't need to start from scratch — ask a freelance friend or find one through an association to tailor to your needs. Editors Canada (editors.ca) has a good contract template. Sometimes a verbal or email agreement is enough; feel out the client's necessity for a contract on an individual basis — if you have any doubts, err on the side of formality: use a contract.

Your contract should list what each party will provide. As the service provider, standard items are: the services that you have promised (and a sense of the scope: remember, how much is included defines what is not included); a timeline for when your project will be completed, including any interim milestones and the final deadline; and details on agreed payment, billing procedures, and payment delivery. Further contract standards include notes about a kill fee (partial payment if the project does not work out), the term of the agreement, procedures regarding cancellation of the agreement, the fact that the writer/supplier is an independent contractor (and therefore not an employee entitled to benefits), and the jurisdiction where the contract should be mediated if necessary. Since the pandemic, a "force majeure" clause has become more common, addressing what will happen if there is an unforeseen event (yes, the unforeseen pandemic, but also fire, explosion, flood, war, government action, strike, and public emergency are listed in one of my recent contracts) and often giving a timeline on what happens after a particular time frame has elapsed, in my example, the client having the right to terminate the agreement in whole or in part.

Contracts are also standard at many magazines, newspapers, and other publications. Unfortunately, contracts still mostly favour big publishers over independent writers. There are quite a few elements within contracts to consider, so I'll just look at three common asks that worry me the most: retaining copyright, keeping moral rights, and not agreeing to indemnification.

To start with, copyright by default is assigned to the author/creator. It belongs to you, and you can choose whether to give it away. Historically, the standard when I started in magazine writing was to sell "first North American serial rights," which means that the publication buys the right to first publish the article, then rights revert to the author. At that point, the author is free to resell the piece if they like.

According to the Canadian Intellectual Property Office, where you can voluntarily register your copyright, copyright is "the exclusive legal right to produce, reproduce, publish or perform an original literary, artistic, dramatic or musical work." No international copyright system exists, but various treaties extend copyright protection to other countries without having to register your copyright in those other countries. Copyright usually belongs to the creator and extends in Canada to seventy years after your death, after which it becomes part of the public domain, which means anyone can use your work.

Now that you know what copyright is, here is why you want to keep it. Read a sample clause below that is becoming more common in contracts:

> First worldwide publication rights including in translation, and the rights to reproduce, transmit, distribute and translate in whole or in part, on magnetic, optical or any other form of electronic media or transmission, whether now in existence or developed in the future, including electronic transmission to online terminals and computer networks for searching, displaying and printing.

As you can see, the above clause limits the right to first rights, meaning that copyright ownership is still with the writer, but the clause tries to see beyond the present by claiming those rights even for technologies "developed in the future." This general paranoia is derived from our ever-changing technological era, where platforms nobody dreamed of are now standard. Publishers think they need to overreach so that they cover themselves for anything in the future. They have also been made overly cautious by lawsuits where freelance writers sued and won the right to a share in the profits that publishers gained by selling work to other companies without first specifically acquiring the rights. Robertson v. Thomson Corp., 2006 SCC 43, is a particularly noteworthy Canadian Supreme Court decision, in which freelance writer Heather Robertson sued the *Globe and Mail* newspaper for unauthorized use of her work in databases where her articles were placed after publication without her permission. The case became a class action suit, and compensation was distributed to freelance writers across the country. Of course, subsequent contracts required freelancers to sign away their rights to keep their work out of these databases.

History repeats itself with these contracts: starting in 2021, singer Taylor Swift began to re-record her own albums as a way of gaining back ownership of the work she had signed away early in her career and which was now owned by new management that was trying to tell her when and where she could play her early songs. Of course, you have to imagine that there's now a clause in record contracts prohibiting re-recordings. Still, fans of copyright like me cheer at the fact that someone who was in a position to fight back did, from Heather Robertson to Swift. Also, Swift's "Taylor's Version" albums reached the number-one position in several countries.

I hope these anecdotes drive home the importance of keeping your copyright. In case they didn't, let me just repeat that as a freelancer, if you sign away your copyright, you no longer own the work. Now, that's already the case if you're working for a traditional employer (employers typically own your work product unless you negotiate a different deal). Yet freelancers, unlike employees, do not get a salary and benefits for their work; thus, they have more of an interest in hanging on to that work, as they could later resell it to another publication or reprint it in a book — both impossible if they no longer own it. Another problem is that publishers who own your copyright have the right to profit from reselling your article. Not that I mind publishers profiting, but if they do, then I want in as well!

Whew, rant over. Wait, one more issue — online rights. Today, a print publication will often assume they are also buying the right to publish your piece online. This used to be negotiated with a separate fee, but with so many publications moving to digital first, it is mostly assumed and included in one fee. Sometimes you can specify the length of time that the piece will stay on the site (six months is a good time frame), and sometimes you can negotiate how long the publication exclusively has the piece or whether you can then sell subsequent rights, although I'd say that online rights are becoming less of a separate negotiable now that many publications are born digital or are digital first. But the bottom line remains: keep your copyright.

Onto an even bigger vampire: moral rights. If you waive your moral rights, you allow a publication to be able to alter the substance or context of your work. In Canada, one of the most famous cases, which also serves as a good visual example of moral rights infringement, involved artist Michael Snow, who created an art installation — *Flight Stop* — of Canada geese hanging as if in flight from the ceiling of the Eaton Centre, a shopping centre in downtown Toronto. Snow sued the Eaton Centre for putting red bows on the geese at Christmas, an addition that he did not approve. Because he kept the moral rights, he was allowed the final say over how they could change his art work, and the mall owners were required to take the bows off. For writers, moral rights protect your reputation in association with the work (in three areas: right of credit or association, right of integrity, and right of anonymity or context, if you want to get technical), so that anyone who wants to change the work has to ask your permission, and so that you can pull your work if it appears in a context that you disagree with (as an extreme example, I often think about what would happen if I wrote a piece for a general newspaper but its database got sold to an online publication that creates content for the tobacco industry, which I do not support). The U.S. does not have the same general legal concept but includes some equivalents — do your research, American friends.

A final worry is an indemnification clause, which shifts the risks or costs from one party to another; it requires the writer to take on their own legal responsibility and cost should someone sue the magazine or client (and the writer) for libel. Historically, the client has taken on this legal responsibility, as they generally have bigger insurance policies. However, I mentioned in an earlier chapter that clients are increasingly asking freelancers to maintain their own professional liability insurance so the organization doesn't need to cover them. Not only are they cutting the freelancer out of the publisher's own coverage, but they are refusing to work with freelancers who don't have coverage. Now, this worry about litigation is more of a problem if you're writing a big investigative story for *Toronto Life* magazine that exposes wrongdoing by a company, and that company is likely to sue you. Not every blog post about widgets is going to meet that threshold, but the spirit of that clause is that the company does not have your back. I now worry less about the indemnity clause because I have purchased my own insurance (a client had refused to cover me anymore, and I wanted to keep working with the client but didn't want to leave myself open to lawsuits), but the clause still makes me feel like the company will never have my back in the case of conflict. However, the fact that I'm seeing this indemnity clause more regularly, that writers are being asked to coordinate their own protection, makes me think it will be standard in a few years.

While these contracts deal with writing that will contain your byline, another type of contract that doesn't necessarily require your byline (or it didn't in the past) is an arrangement called work-for-hire. In this type of work, the client should pay a (much) higher rate — like double — to own the work (or intellectual property) outright. Clients requesting this work-for-hire type of arrangement have traditionally been corporations that might want to use the writing in many different publications or platforms. As long as the writing is so tailored to the client that I can't use it anywhere else, and my byline is removed, I'm usually fine with work-for-hire as long as the pay rate is high enough. Unfortunately, I'm now encountering magazines that include work-for-hire clauses in their contracts and want you to give up your copyright and moral rights while still requiring your byline and without much extra compensation. To this I say no thanks (which is sometimes hard to say when it means giving up a decent client and regular work — but my reputation is everything, and I'm not giving up control over my work that easily).

Unfortunately (I seem to be writing that word a lot in this section), many larger publishers are mercenary on contracts, telling writers to take it or leave it. Desperation for clippings means entry-level writers take the risk and sign the contracts anyway. This endorses publishers to keep using these contracts, and in my opinion, exposes those desperate writers to too much risk. A first line of defence is to actually read your contracts, and make an effort to understand them, either by sharing puzzling clauses with a freelance friend or community or circling back to ask for clarity. Second, challenge clauses — you never know what a client will say, and sometimes they can be flexible. I've heard from many editors and clients that many freelancers never ask. I beg new writers to decline these contracts for their own sake and for the good of the industry. My last "unfortunately" is to say that many writers at any stage are now deciding they don't care about this contract hurdle and are writing under whatever conditions they're asked to — in the example of a recent contract I turned down, which I thought nobody should sign, I was dismayed soon after to see the byline of another freelancer appear, none the wiser to anyone but me that they had given up so much.

Invoicing

On to cheerier topics — collecting your hard-earned money! After you've finished a project, an invoice is your standard format for requesting payment. As a courtesy (particularly with a new client or editor), check in and make sure the project is finished and that it's okay to send your invoice. For publications,

PRICING SERVICES, GETTING PAID

invoices are usually submitted after the first draft has been accepted, although some editors like to wait until the final draft is approved.

Historically, there are a couple of ways to be paid, and fortunately, upon acceptance of the draft has become more standard. Some publications still pay on publication, which is a drag, because if there's a four-month lag between writing the story and its appearance in print, you don't get your fee until then. Try to press for payment on acceptance and send your invoice as soon as you can.

Generally, you invoice after the project is completed, and standard payment terms are usually within thirty days of issuing the invoice, although you can also request payment on receipt (although don't expect to be paid that quickly). For a larger project, say, over $2,000 that will occur over a longer time frame (say, more than three weeks), I will often ask corporate clients to invoice 30 to 50 percent upfront as a deposit. This really helps with cash flow during a project that will go on for weeks, and when you explain that reasoning to clients they can often be understanding. Some freelancers ask for 100 percent upfront, especially when working with a new company where you don't know their cash flow or track record. Some clients (ahem, government) refuse to pay anything upfront, as it doesn't fit with their accounting policies. Try to get the best deal for yourself with a deposit upfront, then see if you want to continue to work for those with long projects that do not pay until the end. If you have expenses — for example, travel to get to an interview — mention and negotiate these upfront and then list them separately on your invoice. I know some freelancers who charge interest on late payments (for example, 2 percent per month). I don't do that, as I'm more likely to follow up after thirty days, but if I had a lot of late payers, I would certainly consider adding interest.

At its most basic, your invoice should contain the date, your name and address, your client's name, a tracking number to be used as a reference (I create mine using the magazine's initials and invoice date; others start at 100 — don't start at 1 or you'll reveal you're a newbie), a short description of the work, your fee plus any GST or HST you are collecting, and your GST or HST number. Don't forget to look up the GST/HST rate if the client is in another province! The invoice looks something like this:

September 1, 2025
INVOICE
To: Jane Smith, Editor, MyFavouriteMagazine
From: Suzanne Bowness, Writer, Address
Invoice #: MFM20240901

    Profile article about important celebrity (1,000 words)

Flat fee	$1,000
HST (13%)	$130
Total	$1,130

THANK YOU.
HST # XXXXXXXXX

Please make etransfers to sue@codeword.ca or make cheques payable to Suzanne Bowness at the mailing address above.

Payable within 30 days.

More clients are moving toward direct deposit (yay!), especially for their regular freelancers, so you should sign up, even though it requires a bit more administration at the start (such as your banking details). I'm still surprised at how many clients still pay by cheque. On the upside, some are starting to skip the accounting department and pay by credit card if you can accept that payment form (you can, with some of the new apps — although they do charge a percentage fee). Some organizations may also issue a tax form (a

T4A here in Canada). Send these slips to your accountant, as it may affect the way you file taxes for that project (for example, list the T4 totals separately from the rest of your freelance income and note if the T4A amounts include GST/HST or not).

Following Up on Payment

If payment seems to be slow, follow up with your editor. I've had a few editors who forgot to pass the invoice along to the accounting department and were extremely apologetic (shortly after is a good time to send in a new pitch while they are feeling indebted to you). If the editor has sent your invoice along and doesn't have any other information, ask for the accounting department's contact details and call them directly. If you have the misfortune of a bad client who is dodging payment, follow up bi-weekly for a couple of months. If you don't get satisfaction, you can send the debt to a collection agency (which, unfortunately, charges a healthy percentage to pursue your debt, but at least you would get something), or you can take a client to small-claims court.

If payment never happens, you can also write the amount off your taxes as bad debt (ask your accountant about this practice). I've had a large company and two start-ups fold and a magazine teeter on the brink. In no case was I, as the freelancer, considered a first-in-line creditor for payouts. On the upside, in twenty-plus years of freelancing, I can count on one hand the number of times that I've had real troubles with payment, so hopefully you won't encounter many difficulties either. I have never taken a client to court for payment (too much hassle and potential cost for too little money), but I have written off bad debt three or four times. Pay attention to organizations that pay too slowly or who are chronically late so you can decide whether or not to keep working for them.

Another phenomenon that happens mostly in writing for publications is that the magazine or client can decide they no longer want your article, either because you didn't deliver what they expected or they've decided to go in another direction, or for reasons unrelated to you. At this time, they should pay you something called a "kill fee." This fee pays you for your time creating the article or assignment and allows you to sell it elsewhere if it's something you pitched. Ideally the fee should be a minimum of 50 percent of what you were set to be paid, or if you're near the end of the assignment, 100 percent. Try to confirm the client or magazine's kill fee policy at the assignment stage if possible, and make sure it is in your contract.

A last note in the money department, repeating somewhat from my business-building chapter but worth restating, is to keep an eye on your business from a financial standpoint. Using either a bookkeeping tool or a simple spreadsheet, track your assignments, payments, and business expenses. When you set yourself income goals, check in monthly to see whether you've met them, and if you haven't, brainstorm ways to catch up, either by sending more pitches or reaching out to regular clients. Over the long term, you may even contemplate whether to look for higher-paying clients or a higher-paying niche, or whether you need a part-time job to make freelancing work.

When you do have a good month, start to put some money aside in your business to balance out leaner months. I keep an emergency fund of around three to six months of expenses so that I'm not worried month over month about how my business is doing. I also have a lower-interest personal line of credit that I can use if clients are late to pay me, to alleviate potential cash flow issues. You can also keep a true personal emergency fund for unexpected expenses, like a big car repair or vet bill. It's not a requirement, but eventually you may want to formalize all of this financial complexity by setting up a business bank account to gain greater separation between your business and your personal finances (some people take this approach from the start). This will be helpful if you're audited as well. All of these proactive actions can help you keep a calm eye on your business finances and ensure that you are aware of where you stand.

BILLABLE TIME

NON-BILLABLE TIME

If the author agrees to move some content from the first chapter to a preface, we could cut a lot of the metadiscourse.

Ohhhh...Did the author mean "commendation" instead of "condemnation"? That would make a lot more sense.

Maybe we could find a way to expand the marine metaphor throughout the text to give it more coherence.

I should confirm which of the images are in the public domain and which ones the author will need permission to reprint.

© Iva Cheung

Chapter 11

Marketing Your Business

Alongside settling into your niche, you should also think long-term about the reputation you want to create — your overall brand. Every writer/editor should have a few basics in their marketing toolkit, including business cards, a website, a LinkedIn profile, and some visibility strategy, often combining social media presence, a newsletter, or other tools for connecting with potential clients. In my informal freelancer survey, when I asked respondents to select all social platforms they use for work, the most popular were

- LinkedIn: 78 percent
- Facebook: 42 percent
- X (formerly Twitter): 33 percent
- Instagram: 30 percent
- Other platforms: 10 percent

Almost 16 percent said they did not use social media (pause for my audible gasp). Regardless of platforms you choose — and your choices should differ by niche — your brand approach should share a common thread by conveying professionalism and a carefully considered work persona rooted in everything from the way your website looks to the way you answer the phone.

For example, whereas most writers will want to maintain a LinkedIn profile, writers catering to a visual industry like architecture or fashion may want to use more visual tools, such as Pinterest, or video platforms like TikTok. Here's where market research comes in, which is to say find out what other freelancers in your niche are doing, and make sure that you at least match the same standard. So, if you are interested in fashion writing, check out what tools the fashion influencers are using and what gets attention within the fashion niche.

Of course, not all of your marketing pieces need to be created at the same time. Start with some basics and plan to add more tools later. It's also better to use two or three tools consistently than to be inconsistent with more. I've met writers who have delayed the start of their business by weeks or months because their business cards were not perfect or their social presence was not polished. Instead, I recommend getting some basics in place on day one — for example, your LinkedIn profile, email signature, and one social platform. Then build the rest, say, your website and other marketing elements, over the first six months. You need to balance creating a presence with getting on with your work.

Marketing also comes in different forms besides tangible print or electronic tools. Networking and, down the road, testimonials and referrals, are equally important to the progression of your business as a freelancer. Now I'm going to go more deeply into some of the elements of your marketing package, both in terms of your tangibles (websites, business cards, social platforms) and your personal outreach (networking and other methods).

Website

Most of your marketing efforts will be online. Editors and clients like to be pitched by email, clients like to see you keeping up a social media presence, and everyone will look for recommendations of your work via a platform like LinkedIn. Your website has replaced the brochure or business card as the central focus of your marketing, and some would argue social media and LinkedIn have eclipsed the writer's website as the main portfolio space.

The reason I like having a website is that I control the content and presentation, and I can centralize links to my presence on all the other platforms that I do not own (read: Twitter turned X, 2023). I may be biased because I boosted my career and got my first internship and my position as online editor on the strength of my HTML wizardry, then made website development an early part of my business. But now simple website development has become much more accessible to the average person; even a non-technical person can set up a decent-looking website using programs like WordPress or SquareSpace, where the interface is fairly intuitive and templates make it easier to select and customize a basic look. My proof of this user-friendliness is the cohorts of students that I've brought through the process for several years via a course I taught on freelancing and portfolio development, some with resistance. Most created a very professional-looking presence.

Here's the paragraph version of my six-week website development course unit: Take a look at other writer's websites for inspiration and you'll see several standard sections: Home, About/Bio, Portfolio, Services, Contact (possibly, you may see Blog). These sections cover what editors and clients want to know: Who are you? What have you done in the past (in other words, what can you show us that's as close as possible to what we want you to do for us)? What services do you offer? How do I get in touch with you? What else shows that you're a person who is in equal measure professional yet easy to work with?

Your website needs to be simple and to clearly guide your visitor to understanding that you're the right person for the job. You'll also want the website to match your brand and, ideally, the industry you're approaching. So, if you're interested in being a financial writer, your look might be a bit more conservative than it would be if you were targeting the music industry with a more creative vibe.

Browse writer websites in your specialty to tailor your look. Once you have created your site, remember to update it quarterly (or before any major outreach) with recent samples and anything else you can think of to convey your brand. For many people, a blog is a great way to share your personal writing style. Ditto social media. Whichever tools or elements you choose, just be consistent — an out-of-date blog or social platform may be worse than none at all.

For editors, websites can be more challenging, as it's harder to share samples given the fact that many clients can be shy about sharing their "before" copy and the copy with your excellent edits. I generally list editing clients but leave samples off my website and note that prospective clients can contact me with requests for samples. That's possibly why editing tests are more common, so employers can see your work in action. But I still stand by websites even for editors because they can share all of the same information as outlined above about their niche, work experience, and a sense of their personality through an About page — all things that can entice a client to try you out.

Brand Consistency

My websites (plural because I have a business site plus an author site for my journalism, speaking, and creative work) are the hub of my business, and I like to use the look and writing style I developed there across my business. I mentioned in an earlier chapter that business cards can still be handy for networking events — I create mine using my website logo along with my email address, phone number, website, LinkedIn profile, and any other platforms I'm using. I keep a short run printed (100–200) for in-person networking events.

Other marketing pieces can depend on the industry that you're targeting. In some industries, postcards can be a memorable piece to leave behind at trade shows. Look around at what others in your niche are trying, or as you get comfortable with your market, experiment with something that makes you stand out in ways that are completely new.

Social Media

Consistency is key for social media. Ideally you registered your business name accounts at start-up, and as you ramp up your business you can decide which platforms to focus on. For all platforms, extend your brand colours and logo as part of your profile. Complete your profile on each platform and make sure you have a decent, professional-looking headshot (ideally the same photo you've used for your website). Include a link to your website in the platform bio and invite contact from potential clients by including your email and the kind of work that you're looking for. As a writer or editor starting out, experiment with different platforms, and after six months, see which you are gaining the most visibility from and meeting the most clients on — and which you enjoy.

As with other elements, a good approach to social media is to see how everyone else in your niche is using it and to balance that with what you're comfortable with. Some are more standard than others; for example, LinkedIn has a pretty strict template, and you should aim to make sure that your profile there is as complete as possible. Set yourself goals in terms of developing your presence on these platforms and see how they work. For the last couple of years, I've written weekly posts for LinkedIn, as an example. My next goal is to interact more.

When new platforms come out (hello, TikTok. Hello, Threads? Mastodon?), definitely look into them and talk to others to find out how they're using them. Then decide whether those platforms would help to get clients, raise your visibility, or connect with your industry. Also decide whether you have time to engage on the platforms and do well. Think about whether you will look behind the times by not being on that platform (feeling my age is what drove me to develop an Instagram presence a couple of years ago, despite not really having a particularly visual business or life). Remember, too, that you don't need to get everything right all at once, so take on only what you can handle and do well.

Networking

When I started freelancing and offered web design as one of my services to other writers and small magazines, I could not believe the number of times I heard a happy client say, "Great, now I'll just put my website online, then clients will google me and I'll be busy!"

Um. It doesn't really work that way.

That is, yes, search engine optimization (SEO) is a thing and you should get your web designer to optimize your space as much as possible, but websites and other marketing materials work best when you use them actively. At minimum, that activity includes appending your website address to your email signature and your pitches and remembering to actually take your business cards with you, not only for professional events but anytime you meet new people, say, at a yoga class or alumni event. You never know who you are going to run into who could use your services.

Successful freelancers also make a point to get out there and meet people in person, even when it seems scary. Regular networking is a long game, although I've also met people at events who needed someone that same week. It's a good thing to plan networking semi-regularly as part of your marketing. So, who do you network with? Start by telling everyone you can think of in your personal circle that you're starting a business. If you've formulated your niche, you'll want to work on an elevator pitch (a term coined for the reason that you should be able to say your idea in the time it would take to complete a medium-length elevator trip — apocryphally by screenwriters in Hollywood trying to pitch to producers).

For example, a health writer might say, "I'm a health writer who writes articles about fitness and nutrition for magazines and marketing materials for hospitals and fitness-related businesses such as yoga studios." Practice your pitch. Say it to everyone: your mom, dad, other relatives, former co-workers, gym buddies, the person sitting beside you on the train, the Facebook friend whom you haven't seen in five years, the alumni coordinator at your university.

After everyone you know is saying, "Yes, we get it, you're a writer/editor," you need to think of other places you can network. One great place to start is other writers' and editors' organizations. In Canada, these include:

- Editors Canada
- International Association of Business Communicators (IABC) — this one is global!
- The Writers Union of Canada (TWUC)

In the United States (with Canadian members), some organizations include:

- American Society of Journalists and Authors (ASJA)
- Editorial Freelancers Association (EFA)
- Society of American Business Editors and Writers (SABEW)
- American Copy Editors Society (ACES)

You can also network with organizations specific to niches or identity groups. To give you a sense of the variety, here are some examples:

- Society for Technical Communication
- Canadian Farm Writers Federation
- Mystery Writers of America
- Crime Writers of Canada
- American Medical Writers
- Asian American Writers Workshop

As you research your niche, you may also want to search whether they have a group already (we writers like to congregate, partly for information sharing and partly because a home office can get lonely). Many of these organizations have local chapters and offer workshops, especially in major cities, and, increasingly, online events too.

Besides networking with other writers and editors, who can be great for professional development and for sharing advice about publications or niches and for commiserating with about the challenges of the writing life, you'll also want to find opportunities to network with potential clients in your niche. Where do they hang out? If they have a professional association, you might consider joining or, at least, attending one of their events. If they have a conference or trade show, consider attending and introducing yourself as a writer. I joined Registered Graphic Designers for a year to get to meet more designers to collaborate with, and it's fun (also intimidating) being the only writer in the room at their conference or on their Slack channel.

Remember, most networking is a soft approach. You're not there to make a sale on the spot but, rather, to meet people, engage potential clients in conversation, and find out how to make their lives easier. For those who fear networking because it seems too forward and/or aggressive, learning that the soft approach is preferable may be a relief, as it makes the practice more palatable. Networkers who aim to hand out as many business cards as possible can actually become notorious; potential clients avoid them.

Since you chose your niche out of interest, demonstrate that fascination by asking questions and starting conversations. Then if you've made a solid connection, that's the time to offer to keep in touch by sharing a business card or searching for your new connections on LinkedIn. After that initial approach, find reasons to reach out to people once in a while — for example, by forwarding an article you think they'll find interesting, or arranging to meet the contact at the next networking event. You might even ask a connection out for coffee or to a Zoom meetup to strengthen the relationship with more face time. A career counsellor I interviewed once for a story on networking described it as a bank account where you should expect to make many deposits before asking for a withdrawal.

Another type of networking emerges once you have clients or editors for whom you write regularly. When possible, try to have coffee (or a video call, post-pandemic) a couple of times a year with a regular editor. Often, they will expect you to bring a couple of pitches to these meetings (you should have your pitches ready even if they didn't ask), and you may be able to get work directly. But primarily, it is a good opportunity to connect with clients on a more personal level. You can even ask to meet with an editor you've only started to connect with and bring pitches there too.

You should also do the same with your regular clients. Make it as easy as possible on clients by offering to meet them close to (or at) their workplace, and offer to pick up the tab if you go out for lunch (coffees and lunches are perfect expenses to write off). Again, being genuine is key to creating a relationship that is professional but friendly.

With the rise of social platforms and with fewer people wanting to meet in person, online networking has become important.

Today, people are showing up particularly on business platforms like LinkedIn. You should too. Start by setting up an all-star profile that includes a carefully written summary, details on each of your past jobs, and a few recommendations/testimonials from people you've worked with in the past.

Begin your online networking by following people and organizations you'd like to work for and observing what they post. Also look for links to post that will be helpful to your connections (I like to share links about writing and marketing, since many in my network are themselves communications professionals). After you've got into a rhythm of observing (I try to go on LinkedIn at least once a day), start contributing (I try to do so weekly on LinkedIn and daily on X, formerly Twitter, although less often now that people are flying that coop). Next step is to look for opportunities to like and comment on other people's posts. All of this effort increases your visibility and, possibly, the chance your name will come to mind next time your connection is thinking about hiring a freelancer. Plus, it contributes to a sense of community.

When you choose platforms, pick those it makes sense to have a presence on (read: where your client base hangs out). So, if you're a design writer, maybe choose Instagram; if you're a scriptwriter, choose TikTok. Schedule time into your calendar for these activities, just like you would any other business task.

Another networking approach that can be a huge benefit is developing a deeper network of freelance friends that you can call on for advice and support (it's called making friends, Sue). Certainly, joining my professional associations and going out to local meetings has been helpful, and if you volunteer for your professional association you can get to know people even better. I also joined a private networking group by invitation (a side benefit of cold outreach, a friendly woman I once connected with said, "I don't have any work for you but why don't you join our freelance group?"). I tried out a paid Mastermind, a structured coaching program that included weekly meetings, one-on-one mentorship, and conferences to work on business development with a group of established freelancers (shout out to the Copywriter Club! Listen to their podcast). One of my favourite and most long-standing networks is one that I started myself. When the private networking group was falling apart (so many retirements ...), I asked my freelance friends that I'd met mostly through volunteering with our professional association if they would like to meet monthly in a "Pitch Club" to work on our businesses. Not all of us are freelance anymore, but we are still writers and friends and still try to meet monthly. They are a great life support, as well as the ones I turn to when I need a safe place to ask my dumbest work-related questions.

Other Promotional Vehicles

As you develop a clientele, you might want to think about places beyond social platforms where you can talk to them. Creating a newsletter can be a great way to stay top of mind with clients, plus share your own writing personality. Decide on a manageable frequency (I do monthly) and send your contacts an invitation to sign up for the newsletter. Create content that your audience will find valuable, and try to make time to include your own original content as well as links sourced from other places.

I started my current CodeWord Communications newsletter with a curated handful of links from twenty-five to thirty marketing websites that I visit weekly (or I now have my assistant visit), and I've since expanded the newsletter to include an original blog post that I also post on LinkedIn. I include links to my latest published work so that my audience can see what I'm working on (and be inspired to hire me for something similar!); I use an online tool called MailChimp to format and schedule the newsletter, and I include a signup in my email signature as well as inviting new clients directly. At the same time I started the Feisty Freelancer website, I also developed a newsletter for freelance creatives! Visit feistyfreelancer.com to sign up.

As you move along in solidifying your business, start looking for other opportunities to reach your clients. Many writers' organizations maintain directories where you can post a profile and a link to your website — for example, Editors Canada (editors.ca). If you've attended an event in your niche, like a trade show, you could consider advertising in their magazine or on their website. For example, in the human-resources niche, where I have written, there is an annual conference with hundreds in attendance and a magazine. You might even consider volunteering to speak at an industry event. For example, if you are a technology writer, that industry has many conferences. Pitching yourself as a guest for a podcast in your niche is a good idea, and so is developing a podcast yourself to share your own thought leadership (try guesting first, as making a podcast is a lot of work!). Whatever you do, try to pick visibility vehicles that you can sustain and, ideally, that you also enjoy.

Referrals and Testimonials

After you've completed a few successful projects, you can also start to access one of the best promotional tools out there: other people's recommendations. Referrals, where someone else recommends you directly to a client, and testimonials, where someone writes something nice about you and allows you to post it in a public place, are among your strongest tools. When someone compliments your work and you feel confident that they're genuinely pleased, that's the time to ask for a testimonial.

Fortunately, a function on LinkedIn has made testimonials increasingly easy to ask for and straightforward to provide. If you feel equally confident about recommending your client or editor, you may also offer to write a reciprocal testimonial. When you do, try to be concrete (ideally your contact will do the same). Instead of writing "Anna is a very good editor," write "Anna is a skilled editor who provides detailed assignment letters and was always available for follow-up questions during the course of our project."

Referrals can happen spontaneously when a satisfied client passes on your name, but you should get in the habit of asking for them directly. When you've completed several projects and you're confident you've done good work, ask your client if anyone else within the client's organization, or even in their circle of contacts, could use your services (and would they mind connecting you). Remember that it never hurts to make yet one more person aware that you're looking for new business.

Of course, when you get a referral, you'll want to reach back and say thank you. If it's appropriate, and especially if it's a colleague or fellow freelancer who has passed you the work, a small gift (coffee gift cards are perfect for this thank-you gesture) can be a tangible way to show your appreciation.

Brand *You*

As a final word on marketing, I think an equal part of branding is to create a set of standards that you will try to stick to as a service provider. When it comes to projects, my minimum standards are (a) always meeting my deadlines (or if I must miss, offer as much notice as possible), (b) being easy to work with (no diva behaviour), and (c) producing the work that I've been asked for (don't submit 1,500 words if I've been asked for 1,000). And remember, your excellent work is also your calling card, so (d) keep pitching great ideas and coming up with stories that surpass expectations.

Other brand standards are more personalized but should generally match the professionalism you've already established. For instance, I try to answer emails within twenty-four, if not twelve, hours; to keep my social media presence active; to reach out to clients on a semi-regular basis (at least quarterly, if not more often); and to keep in touch with editors if a project is going off the rails beyond my control. All of these elements are equally, if not more important than how shiny your website looks or how sassy you sound on social media.

Exercises

EXERCISE 1

Brainstorm your brand. What kind of writing would you like to do? What image would you like to project and how would it fit with the sector that you are interested in? Are there any colours, designs, or logos that you see for yourself? Ask yourself some of the major branding questions that brand experts will ask organizations to come up with: If you were an established brand like Apple or Coke, which one would you be? If your brand were an animal, what would it be? If your brand had a song, what would it be? Analyze your choices. Have fun with it!

EXERCISE 2

Look at two or three websites for writers in a niche you've been contemplating. How do they express their brand? What experience do they share that would appeal to editors in their niche? What samples do they share that point to common forms in this niche? Do those forms interest you?

Chapter 12

Staying Motivated While Working from Home

For many years, I've been telling people that one of the reasons I enjoy freelancing is the total control over my schedule. Grocery shopping at quiet times in the middle of the day, putting on a load of laundry between interviews, and sidestepping any questions about the amount of tea I drink in a day because nobody can witness all my trips to the kitchen are all perks of twenty-plus years in a home office.

But just like my students, who have to do a thing for themselves before they believe what I've told them about it, nobody in traditional office jobs really appreciated my plug for the freelance lifestyle until the pandemic hit. Now everybody wants to work from home (WFH).

I first wrote this chapter during the pandemic as a general guide for any worker finding themselves in lockdown. I posted it on the feistyfreelancer.com website along with a collection of links on the topic. People new to this lifestyle were asking all kinds of questions, and their thoughts on the topic were similar to mine. I also learned about some of the unique challenges that stemmed from adjusting to a home office and the particular challenges that parents faced in working from home while also schooling from home.

Of course, working from home during a lockdown is a more particular stress given the pandemic nightmare. A writer meme making the rounds at the time joked that even the introverts were saying, "This was not what we meant by saying we didn't particularly enjoy socializing." Since this is a book for the freelancers in the room, I'll focus there, although a lot of these tips apply equally to those lucky workers who get both the WFH flexibility and a rock-solid salary (less lucky are the workers who face heavy monitoring by their employers).

Work-from-Home Attitude

For people who set out to work from home as freelancers, one of the first adjustments is to your attitude. In order to make a living being self-employed or running your own business, it's important to take yourself seriously. I've already addressed the mindset issues of calling yourself a writer and dealing with impostor syndrome, but the adjustment to freelancer bears repeating.

The best advice I have for taking your freelancer lifestyle seriously is to put routines in place that help you take your work seriously. By extension, everyone else will too. For me, some of those elements include establishing a permanent work station in my home, setting a structure for my day, and establishing other routines that help to make me feel like I'm in a workplace even when it's in my home. Let's walk through each of these areas.

Finding a Space

Finding a space to work makes a difference in how you spend your workday. If you have a room, say, a spare bedroom, that you can turn into your home office, set up there. If you don't have that luxury of space, find a corner, whether it be a corner of your bedroom or a section of your living room, that you can turn into an office. Preferably this workspace should be permanent so you can leave and return to it as if you are entering an office. After all, what is an office but the place where you store your computer?

Ideally this space is comfortable, with decent lighting, a good supportive chair, a flat surface for your computer, and low traffic if you are working with family members nearby (you could even make a sign to tell passersby when this office is in session). Ideally you are faced away from the centre of the room and other distractions. Noise-cancelling headphones can help. Add a desk lamp, a bottle of water, and all your tools, including pens, sticky notes, and reference books within reach. Once you've found and built your space, communicate to everyone in your household that it's not to be touched and that you're not to be bothered there, except in case of urgent need (such as occasional feline calls for tummy rubs). Having this space to go to and walk away from mimics the commute to work and helps to develop physical separation between your home and workspace.

I also love extra tools that make my office even more enjoyable. Probably my best upgrade in the last five years was a second monitor (trash-picked off the curb; these upgrades don't need to be expensive). A close second was a bigger desk. I also got a kneeling chair so I can mix up my sitting situation for my tricky back. Some people love standing desks. Some people like those yoga balls to balance on. Everyone should find what they like and think about ways to improve the eight daily hours they spend in their home office space. I like sitting near a window and having an overhead light as well as task lighting (which doubles as my video conference light). My bookcases with my dictionary and style guides are nearby, as are a three-tier filing tray and magazine holder. I like having plants on my desk and cat colleagues to wander in and out.

Speaking of spaces, not all have to be in your home. While home offices have been embraced since the pandemic, before that, co-working spaces had been growing in momentum. I joined a co-working space for a bit and really liked the vibe of quietly working with businesses that were similar to mine. They also offer boardroom-style spaces that you can book for client meetings. Some freelancers I know visit these spaces even more often, from two or three times a week to taking an office full-time at the co-working space. Factors that can influence this choice include the need for more separation between work and home (sometimes because of kids or a spouse who is also working from home), to make space when there isn't a room in your home, and to create networking opportunities (my co-working space had regular weekly meetups where you could socialize with other business owners, and not all were writers, so you could even peddle your services!).

Key to making co-working spaces productive is finding a space convenient enough that you'll actually use it (sounds like my rules for a gym membership).

Structuring Your Day

Whereas the work-from-home office worker has a structure imposed on them by their workplace employer, a perk and challenge for us self-employed people is imposing structure on ourselves. Of course, during different phases of your life, regular hours might not be available, so you might need to shorten these or set others' expectations. For instance, those with young children might set work hours after bedtime or before their kids wake up. Some parents work while kids are at school, ending their workday in time for the after-school pickup. Experiment with the number of hours that works for you and the others in your life who need your attention.

Another element particular to the work-from-home life where a freelancer is making work out of thin air (or so it may seem to your loved ones) is the need to teach people to respect your office hours. When I started my business, I told friends and family that I was not available from 9:00 a.m. to 5:00 p.m. and they mostly took me seriously, except for the occasional call in the middle of the day. One trick that I use is to answer my phone during the weekday with "Hello, Sue speaking" as an added reminder (to myself as well as others). I've told everyone in my circle that I screen my calls and will ignore them if they call when I am doing an interview or am on a tight deadline. When people suggest taking time off during my workday, I will often plan to meet them at the end of the day so that I've got in most of my hours beforehand, and I limit any longish networking lunches to once or twice a month because they can be really disruptive to the flow of my day.

Setting hours when you'll be at work also means setting hours when you'll be away. You teach people how to treat you when you're always available for work, and while our online culture sets an expectation to be online 24/7, remember that it's an individual choice to check email and social at any time of day. I try to limit my evening check of work email to once or twice after 6:00 p.m. and not after 9:00 p.m. I set expectations by letting clients know that I'm not going to reply to work emails too far outside of work hours or much on the weekend (I've set these limits with my night-owl students too).

I've noticed this way of thinking is finally catching on, as many email signature tags now acknowledge "my work hours may not be your work hours" — a sign of progress.

As a final note, it's not just setting expectations for other people but for yourself — the upside-down version of working-from-home freedom is that you live at work all the time, feeling like you should just go in and add something to a project or do one more hour. If you return to your desk repeatedly, it will feel like you never get away. If you find yourself being an evening-and-weekend workaholic, try writing a reminder note about the nagging task on your phone or calendar, just like you would if you were going to a real workplace — the idea is captured, but you can go on with your evening.

Dress for Your Day

Another set-up aspect may be your self-presentation, i.e., getting dressed and showered. Freelancer pro tip: do it. I find when I'm presentable, I take myself more seriously. This goes double in our current age of conference calls, where you're expected to look professional at least from the waist up (another pandemic lesson: you really can wear leggings all day long!). Being ready for the day also means that you won't be caught off guard by that unexpected video call.

Your personal prep could include dressing up with full makeup (or beard fully oiled), or whatever else helps you feel professional. I have read about people who leave their house and take a walk around the block because it helps them get in the mood to arrive at their home office.

Set Your Breaks

If you tend toward workaholism like I do, leaving work at home can be the hard part — when I first started freelancing, I used to schedule a yoga class for the end of some workdays to provide myself a hard stop. Even now, if I'm working past 5:00 p.m., I schedule a walk or other break so returning to work afterward is an active decision and not just a day-fades-into-night slippery slope.

Almost as important as setting hours is setting break times. I try to move and stretch once an hour and make plenty of pots of tea as an excuse. My lunch break mostly involves a half-hour of television. I cannot recommend enough the power of a full-stop half-hour lunch away from your desk to refresh the mind. In my world, an hour feels like too much of a luxury, but no lunch break feels unthinkable (unless in the face of a tight deadline). Others more virtuous than me prefer a midday walk or workout. If you adopt this lunch-break policy and then return to the traditional workplace, please take it back to the office with you so we can normalize it. I wonder sometimes if the urge in traditional workplaces to work from home is just so the employees can take back their lunch breaks sight unseen.

Yet another aspect of structuring your workday while working at home is deciding what non-work you will do during working hours. For me, it's yes to a quick laundry break, mostly no to outside errands unless I am out for a meeting and tack it on after. Dishes sit in the sink, shelves go undusted, and personal phone calls mostly go unreturned during my workday. If you can't face that chaos, then build tidying into your personal time to keep your living space from being a distraction. Or literally don't face the living space — as a freelancer friend said, "Turn your desk to the wall so you can't see the mess." Now that's discipline. That's not to say I don't take the occasional afternoon off. I have shared with my students my "Freelancer Friday" matinee ritual — key to my awesome life as an independent worker. But otherwise, I am mostly at my desk during working hours.

Communicating

Communications become even more important when working from home. Because you're often dialing in as the contractor on the project, you can be overlooked or seem further away than others who are face-to-face in a meeting room. Those of us who have been zooming in for years know it can be a struggle to be seen. When you don't have a cubicle down the hall from a colleague, you need to take extra steps to remind them virtually that you are also available. One way I combat this proximity challenge is to over-communicate: I provide unsolicited updates or check-ins every few days on long-term projects; I also make sure my voice is heard on video conference calls even if it is just to clarify takeaways and confirm my understanding of my role or a to-do list. Again, a minor upside of the pandemic (I try not to use the words "pandemic" and "upside" in the same sentence) is that people are more familiar with working from home and finally realize that people who are out of office can be just as much a part of the team.

Asking people for their preferred means of communication and making sure you're on that channel can also be helpful. When new clients ask if I can use their conferencing platform, my first answer is yes, and then I do a quick internet search to find out how. Participating on any platform as requested helps to show you're open to collaboration and new technology. Do be open to technology — don't be the person who groans or resists a new tool. You may even want to be proactive and suggest tools that you've found helpful (freelancers are good at this tech-tool awareness, as they work for many clients and by necessity know many tools). If someone invites you to the Slack channel, sign up for the Slack channel. Proof that I walk this talk is found in the fact that I recently joined the chat app Discord upon request.

When you're working from home for the first time, schedule time to familiarize yourself with these new platforms and practice with a friend so that you're able to be professional when called on. If you are supervising people working from home, the communications tactics go both ways: find out how your employees like to communicate and establish your expectations clearly if you want to use a particular tool. Be open to suggestions about platforms and be patient as employees adjust to new tools.

Managing Your Workload — A Closer Look

Find the work, do the work, repeat. Set goals and assess what is the right balance of work for you. See what projects you find the most fun. And profitable. Analyze your energy levels to make the most of your day. These are a few habits to get into, ones that lead to routines. Over years of doing so, here's what mine look like.

A DAY IN THE LIFE
Writing this on a Monday, I spent the first half-hour of my workday looking at a handful of job sites that I check weekly for potential new gigs, including Jeff Gaulin's Journalism Job Board, the Quill & Quire job board, and Charity Village (see more resources in Appendix A), then a half-hour responding to email and sending some others to set up interviews for another project. Then I had breakfast mid-morning (tasty sesame seed bagel!), followed by a Zoom interview at 11:00 a.m. for an article. While the interview was still fresh in my head, I wrote a quick draft of the article (a shorty), then I went back to a project I'd finished on Friday (a multi-part editing project!) to look at it with fresh eyes before I sent the draft in.

After a lunch-and-TV break, I conducted an interview at 2:00 p.m. that was quite technical. The interviewee was a bit reluctant, and dragging the content out of her left me feeling a bit stressed, so I took another break afterward to decompress. But I soon realized I should write a quick (rough) draft of that article while some of the technical details were on my mind. Then I started a ghostwriting assignment for a new client that I'll look at again tomorrow, as it is quite rough, although I'm glad I at least got started. Then the cats began to paw at the office door for dinner; I needed dinner too, and now it's evening.

In terms of the ways that working from home impacted this schedule, it's the fact that I decided on what to do and when that makes being self-employed different from being in an office. I still needed to attend the meetings that I had organized, but I could take breaks around those meetings to manage my energy. I could take a longer break after the harder interview without anyone asking why I felt I needed to watch the whole episode of the renovation show rather than my usual half. I usually break at 5:00 p.m., but on this day I worked until 6:00 p.m. to make up for my longer afternoon break.

A WEEK IN THE LIFE

Generally, I plan my week around meeting assignment deadlines. At the same time, my next week(s) will be pretty quiet if I don't do some outreach for new projects, so I also plan for later. People who work for one workplace may not have to pitch in the same way, but you might also plan to refresh your relationships with colleagues.

If I have three articles due in a week, I try to plan the amount of time needed for each and see what prep is required before I start — for instance, emailing or calling someone who might not be available immediately. I may also plan to start a different article each day so I am fresh for each new writing session, as well as leave some space before each actual project deadline for proofreading. I schedule in administrative tasks like invoicing, updating my website, and work-related reading. These can also fit between the larger assignment deadlines either as a break or as a way to task-switch when I'm getting tired of my article. As I mentioned when discussing productivity, rote tasks like invoicing are good candidates for batching, as I don't want to switch between tasks too quickly. At the end of the week, I think about how I did and what I might do differently next time to be even more efficient.

My previous week looked like this: it was my usual nine to five at my desk, but on Tuesday I was invited to give a (paid) talk to a class about writing, so I took the afternoon off and rather than coming back to my desk, I took advantage of being close to a mall and ran some errands. The next day, I extended my hours because I felt a bit behind on my tasks for the week. On Friday, I scheduled an oil change for my car at 11:00 a.m. and took my laptop to Tim Horton's (unusual for me to work elsewhere), where I was surprisingly productive in editing an article for an annual report I was working on.

A MONTH IN THE LIFE

Over a month, I typically write two to four feature stories in the 1,200- to 2,000-word range, a handful of shorter articles in the 400- to 800-word range, and a bunch of corporate assignments in the 500- to 1,000-word range. I may copy edit or proofread one or two documents, mostly reports but everything from brochures to case studies. Other projects include website content, media releases, emails, media kits, and many other forms. (I was once hired to write a greeting card, both my highest-paying and lowest-wordcount gig ever: eight words at $5 a word.)

To keep myself organized over the month, I keep a spreadsheet of my tasks, pitches, and deadlines. I also keep a list of long-term projects, such as writing this book, refreshing my website, and pursuing a new client base. My ideal is to get work done on these long-term items every week (sometimes it comes to just looking at the long-term to-do list). I typically use Friday afternoons for these big-picture tasks. For a goal that veers into lower-paid passion project territory (see: book proposal), I will sometimes even work on a weekend morning. Keeping a log of how you spend your time (there are good apps to help with this time-tracking) can give you insight on where you can be more efficient. I recently started using a time-tracker to see how often I'm distracted by email!

As mentioned, I try to spend most of my workday, from nine to five, butt-in-seat at my desk. I take advantage of the freedom to do grocery shopping, make car appointments, and meet friends for the occasional networking lunch, although I try not to do that more than one day per week. If it's a day or week with a lot of deadlines, I will often work later one evening or start earlier one morning to make up some time. I try not to work on weekends, but I'm not terribly upset if I have to finish a project on a Saturday morning, especially if it means feeling more relaxed about my upcoming week.

A YEAR IN THE LIFE

Working from home is fairly stable once you're into it, but a year in the WFH lifestyle can offer ways to work away from home. I'm talking about the ability to plan and take vacations without approvals, to take afternoons off, and to focus some weeks on special projects (like finishing this book!). While your decisions are your own, the effort does take some planning. I've mentioned that I often schedule vacations when my editors are off too. I often check email while I'm away, whether for the afternoon or even on holiday — just to make sure that I don't miss out on work opportunities (some freelancers have a stricter policy on this freedom and switch off everything; fortunately, as independents, we can all do what we like!).

Ideally I try to plan time off when work has tapered, and I arrange for deadlines to fall a bit before or after my holiday. Or I will tell the client that I'm taking time off (a couple of weeks before) and, especially if we're in the middle of a project, come up with a plan to manage the workflow so that my holiday is not too disruptive to a project. Clients appreciate that workaround, and I think of it as another element of building a good reputation.

I mentioned that Friday afternoons are my monthly times to work on my business, but occasionally I take an entire afternoon or two per quarter to check in on my goals and tweak anything that's not working. I will also attend one or two writing conferences per year as a way of inspiring myself and my business, plus tack some travel onto my conference trip if the event is in an interesting new destination.

So, that's my WFH life. Most workdays are spent at my desk, and most evenings and weekends are off. The big difference is that the office panopticon is not there monitoring me, so I can feel free to wander around and wring my hands when I'm feeling impatient with a story, or take a longer break during the day, or work late without questions. As a freelancer, you set your own expectations, and your deadlines are not set for you, so you have the autonomy to schedule as you wish. Of course, this autonomy can be upside and downside. But I've found that it works well for me!

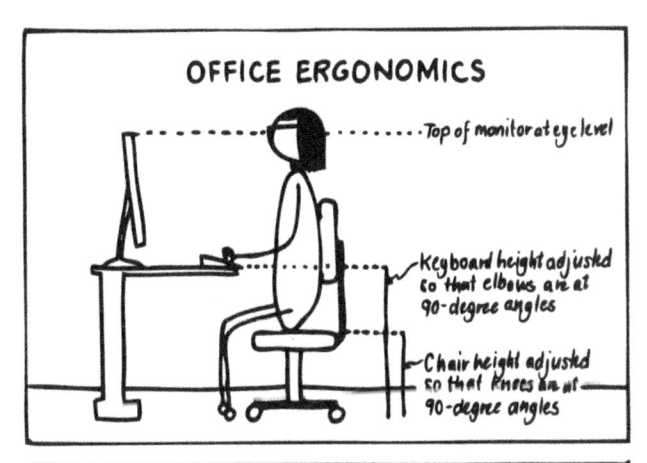

OFFICE ERGONOMICS
- Top of monitor at eye level
- Keyboard height adjusted so that elbows are at 90-degree angles
- Chair height adjusted so that knees are at 90-degree angles

HOME OFFICE ERGONOMICS
- No fewer than three pillows
- Laptop with >3 hours of battery power
- Reliable WiFi connection
- Pants: optional

© Iva Cheung

Chapter 13

Advancement Strategies for Successful Freelancers

Starting a full-time freelance business requires patience in terms of finding clients and establishing routines but also in finding success. In my first year, I didn't make that much money, even though I was working hard (let's just say, it was a good thing I had a roommate to share the rent). When you start freelancing, plan to have an unpredictable ramp-up. In that first year, everything felt a bit slow and dumb, and looking back I was making many mistakes or doing things inefficiently, both because the tasks were new to me and because I was figuring out my business.

Hopefully, this book will help you skip a few early mistakes, but at the same time you need to have patience with yourself. Ideally before starting you'll have saved a buffer of money (six months if you can — although when I was laid off I got two months of severance) so that you're not constantly worrying. I've mentioned trying freelancing part-time so that you know what you're getting into. But eventually you'll go full-time, and eventually you'll finish your first year and look back on the fact that you supported yourself through writing, and that will feel great (even if supporting yourself meant having to eat ramen noodles more nights a week than you'd admit to your friends). After a few years of freelancing, I looked around my apartment with pride, thinking *I bought all this (mostly second-hand) furniture with my writing!* (I still look around my living space and am equally proud that the furniture has seen a slight upgrade.)

Then in the second and third year, you'll figure out a few more things about how you work best, you'll find that some great clients are calling you back, and each year you'll make a bit more money until your income and schedule is more predictable. And you'll do that year over year.

And year over year over year over year over year over year over year.

And that's fine. Just like in a traditional workplace, you can stay in a job for many years, maybe even your whole career, and the variety of projects, the people you work with, or the work itself will be enriching and sustaining and fun. You can set yourself great goals like landing a feature assignment for a high-profile magazine, editing for a dream client, writing for your favourite non-profit, or adding editing to your list of skills if you're a writer, and vice versa if you're an editor.

But in a traditional workplace, maybe there will be a point when you think, *I'm good at this and I like this, but ... what else could I do?* You might start looking to move up the ladder or to make a lateral move into a different department or even to a different company.

And you might have these thoughts about freelancing too.

Except freelancing is a little different. Because there aren't really senior freelancers. I tell my students, half-joking but mostly serious, that with a good story idea they can vault the queue over a long-time freelancer like me to land a feature in a prestige magazine that I've always wanted to write for.

Yet besides the power of a great idea, experience matters. Over time, your writing will improve to the point where you are consistently landing work as a writer and your first drafts are consistently passable. You'll be a sharper editor with many years of experience. If you're a career professional just turning freelance, you're there already.

So, what other things can you do with your business? Here are a few ideas.

Specialize Even Further

I mentioned that your skills may plateau at a certain point, but you can also develop specialty skills that most writers don't have; that upskilling can edge you toward higher rates or put you in a category of one as a freelancer with very in-demand credentials. For example, some freelancers who work with a lot of financial clients take the Canadian Securities Course (CSC), a financial exam that allows professionals to sell mutual funds but also provides a foundational grounding that can help you understand and tell more technical stories. Speaking of technical writing, that's a thing; writers take courses in that area to be in demand by software companies and others that require manuals and documentation.

If you're good with languages, you might upgrade your skills to be able to offer bilingual writing, editing, or even translation services (truly a strategic move in bilingual Canada). You could take a couple of courses in the medical field that qualify you for more lucrative work as a medical writer or editor. Any of these niches are not as accessible to the standard generalist writer/editor and put you into a smaller hiring pool with higher potential compensation.

As an editor, consider studying for one of Editors Canada's certification exams, rumoured to be quite challenging but an excellent way to develop professionally, validate your skills, and stand out among other professionals. I know several writers who have taken college certificates in social media topics to add to their service offerings. Over the years, I have taken courses in copy editing, graphic design (I still consider InDesign as wizardry, but at least I know more about it), and proofreading, as well as a self-paced online course in Indigenous history (when I started to work for universities with larger Indigenous populations). There are many online courses available for free, including from Coursera and Udemy or LinkedIn Learning, to help raise your skills on topics from search engine optimization to Google analytics to integrating AI. Attending writing and editing conferences is also helpful to learn about niche areas that can fill in knowledge gaps.

With further learning either independently or through a course, you can also specialize just by writing exclusively in one area and becoming known as the go-to person, again a strategy to make you in demand. For example, if you specialize as a copywriter for coaches who launch courses, professionals in that niche are going to queue up to hire you. As another example, once you've specialized as an email sequence copywriter, you might create your own courses to teach in your specialty or write a book (or several) in the niche (such as parenting) to further cement your authority. As an editor, you could add another niche to your portfolio; for example, editor Iva Cheung added cookbook editing to her other skills in plain language editing.

These activities not only make you more exclusive as a writer or editor, but the challenges may also make your working life more fun and interesting.

Or Add a New Niche

I started out freelancing by pitching to magazines in the technology niche because I've always been curious about gadgets, especially the way they help the average human. At the time, the tech boom of the early 2000s was still in play, so there were lots of options. Once I'd been freelancing in tech for a while, some opportunities in business more broadly came up, so I added those topics to my repertoire. Then an opportunity to write for a human-resources magazine turned into a niche in that area.

As I was completing my Ph.D., I realized that I could turn my newfound knowledge of the academic realm into a client base. Oh, and burying the lede here, I also did a Ph.D. because writing my Master's thesis was intriguing, and taking that further sounded interesting and had potential to boost my teaching career. At the same time, I've taken my niches with me — for example, even as I write stories for education magazines, I'm always pitching or being offered the stories with a bit of a technical focus. So, if there's a niche that intrigues you, and especially if it seems like a growing area, that can be a great addition and can keep your writing business interesting.

Seek Out Management Opportunities

In traditional jobs, the climb up the corporate ladder often leads to management roles. You get good at the work and start to manage and mentor teams of others who are honing their skills, providing them feedback and mentorship. Then you might find yourself leading projects or even ascending to lead divisions of the organization, planning and visioning how they will grow.

As a (technically, by years invested) senior freelancer, you can also start pitching yourself into these management opportunities. For example, advertise that you are available not only to write for the magazine but to be its editor, handling everything from managing freelancers to editing copy and working with designers to coordinate the layout. You can team up with designer colleagues to pitch entire projects, such as annual reports, again where you'll coordinate collecting the copy and editing it into a single voice, and your designer will coordinate layout and image selection.

When you're pitching to take on these bigger projects, look for elements that are less entangled in the day-to-day work of the company, where you can make the argument that taking those tasks off their plate can save the communications team time. Sometimes these projects are even advertised in Requests for Proposals (RFP); the organization has already made the move to hive off the project and all you need to do is bid (I say this like it's easy; typically, these processes are quite competitive).

You can also pitch yourself as a more management-level business owner — for example, instead of calling yourself a social media writer or coordinator, call yourself a social media strategist or consultant, where your main task is visioning and planning the year's social media, and either you or the company's internal team can work on bringing the content to life. As a consulting editor, you can advise on a magazine's start-up phase and leave the project to a managing editor once it is operational. These strategist roles require a greater understanding of the audiences, goals, and vision for the business so command a higher compensation level as well as a more senior-level understanding of social media or magazine planning than content creation.

If you've already built a traditional career in one of these areas and have management experience, point to this work you've done in the past and the fact that you're now just pivoting to freelance. Think about ways to create a package that includes your strategy plus content creation, either priced monthly or quarterly, to organize your skills into a single offering. For example, as a social media strategist you might include a strategy plan plus a monthly retainer for managing the platforms of a small business. If you're a marketing specialist, a job title I see popping up more often now is a "fractional Chief Marketing Officer."

Because this work calls on organizations to trust an external provider, I do find it can be harder to access. Many organizations like to keep their strategy internal and farm out content creation. Some are willing to assign the annual report content but want the manager to be in-house. Some will assign the magazine articles but stop short of allowing a consultant to develop the content lineup. So even as a senior freelancer, you may still find yourself doing a lot of content work. But the more strategy you pitch for and complete, the more samples you'll have to refer to, and referrals may come your way. Plus, I still like content creation, as it keeps me fresh and close to my original love of writing, so I wouldn't want to give it up no matter how senior I am.

Develop an Agency

If you're interested in management, another route is to manage your own writers and develop an agency. With junior writers and even senior partners, you can take on larger clients, more work, and different types of projects. By the time you are thinking about starting an agency, you may already have worked with a few and have a sense of the sorts of projects they do. Consider meeting with a couple of agencies that you've worked with as a writer. Ask agency leaders about their routines, how they pitch, and how they manage their projects. Often, a good place to meet this type of mentor is through an industry association, where you can find a lot of goodwill to share knowledge after you've built enough of a relationship.

A good way to test the waters might be to hire an assistant and see how it feels to hand off work to another team member, train them, and answer their questions. You can also try hiring a junior writer on a larger project and see how you work with others, providing direction and feedback. Even if you decide to stay solo, the exercise can help you to think about benefits to bringing others into your business.

When I hired an intern for a summer, I created some standard operating procedures for elements of my business — documents that outlined how things are done — essentially moving procedures from deep in my brain and muscle memory to the page.

I experimented with writing the procedures myself but found it equally helpful to have my intern create them, and then one of us filled in the blanks the other left out. Now my procedures for social media posting, invoicing, and client management are all documented, so when I hire a new assistant, I don't have to pause and explain what I do. I can just reference those documents.

While I've kept my freelance business mostly tight at the solo-plus-assistant model, occasionally hiring junior writers for bigger projects, I've thought a lot about the agency model. Definitely there are upsides, such as the ability to work on bigger projects with higher income potential and the chance to do interesting work. The downsides are possibly less flexibility given that you're now responsible for other employees and the worry that comes with being accountable for their livelihoods, plus the need to find those bigger projects that can sustain you. But this growth can also be exciting. Even moving away from the core skills of writing in favour of more project management is a consideration with pluses and minuses (as for any senior employee).

Try Teaching Your Skill

One way that I have kept my writing life interesting is by teaching. This has worked well for my business in several ways: teaching a couple of courses per term gives me regular income and takes a bit of the pressure off freelancing. Teaching is compatible with freelancing given that control over your schedule means even daytime classes can be easy to fit in. And it's fun to pass along your passion for the industry to a new generation that is freshly enthusiastic. I also find that articulating my skill makes me better at the skill by having to explain things I did automatically. Let's say I watched a lot of grammar videos on YouTube that first year.

While you don't need a Ph.D. to teach (although I did find a great dissertation topic exploring nineteenth-century Canadian magazines), look around for colleges or universities near you that may have a writing program, and connect with the staff in charge of the program (usually, Program Coordinator is the right title to reach out to). Let them know you're available and the topics you feel most able to teach (look at the course list to identify which offerings resonate). I have to say that "sessional" (term by term) teaching has its downsides, namely, the pay is low for the number of hours you put in (you're paid for the classroom hours but not for the vast marking and preparation), but it can also be a good option for a senior freelancer looking to mix it up. Some writers even transition fully to teaching.

Develop a Side Hustle

If you suddenly find yourself a senior freelancer because you secretly or not so secretly love the hustle of entrepreneurship (hello!), then you may think about ways to do new things in business. Just because you're a writer doesn't mean you can't develop a side hustle or a totally different business simultaneously.

This can happen at any stage: I started out my business as two offerings, Code+Word, because I knew HTML, and I created thirty-five to forty websites for other writers in the first three years of my business as I grew my writing clientele. I eventually wound down that second part of my business when I felt more confident about my workflow as a writer (and less confident about conducting an online business where I felt like I could get sued if anything went wrong).

So, if you're a writer with a passion for fashion styling, why not try fashion styling? Or if you are fascinated by illustration, or indexing, or jewellery making, those can all be compatible side hustles (I've met writers with all of these side hustles as part of their work life). Or start your own newsletter or magazine if you want to stay within the editorial realm? If the benefit for a writer is a flexible workday, the choice to turn that flexibility to another business is up to you.

If you've embraced the flexibility of freelancing for the ability to take on more hobbies or passion projects, whether it be writing your novel or starting a non-profit or volunteering at your local women's shelter, a more established, stable business can be the time to look at your workload and see how you can make that work. Maybe you have to find higher-paying clients so that you make your same salary with fewer hours. Or restructure your workday to allow you to carve off a day per week for your novel.

The only thing I suggest is not to do business for free or cheaply when other people are trying to actually make a living at it. I say this because as side hustles have become a thing, "content writing" pops up as a suggestion in articles on top side-hustles, along with the note that "it's easy to get into." I know these content side hustlers are likely not charging market rates and are bringing the industry down as a result. I think, *Hey! Your side hustle is my hustle!*

So, whether you're after a side hustle or a different way of freelancing, there are lots of options; with control over your own time, you have the power to try them out. Or not. You can also just enjoy your lovely freelance life with lots of flexibility. I love that freelancing gives me more time to work on creative writing, for example, and move that interest forward. Whatever you decide, just know that you have options and you are in charge.

ADVANCEMENT STRATEGIES FOR SUCCESSFUL FREELANCERS

© Iva Cheung

Chapter 14

AI and the Future of Freelancing

In January 2023, I made my first serious exploration (read: afternoon of experimentation) of the new ChatGPT generative artificial intelligence (AI) tool released the previous fall. I'd been reading lots of articles and listening to podcasts about it, plus chatting nervously with other writer colleagues about its potential impact on our work. After all, the tool was rumoured to be able to write the types of blog posts that were one of my staples, only in a fraction of the time.

I first tried writing a poem for my bi-weekly poetry group, both to start a conversation and because little old human me was behind in producing her contribution. I asked ChatGPT to write a poem with the cheeky title, "The End of Poetry," and the result was pretty laughable. Turns out the tool's default form was rhyming couplets, which to us serious types was very grade two–level poetry. Then I asked ChatGPT to write without rhyming couplets, and it just wrote a different rhyming couplets poem. But a couple of the couplets were pretty good. Another poet friend turned up with the same experiment, but she had input her own poem and asked the machine to rewrite it. Again, much of it was worse than the original, but a couple of lines were good. Hmm.

This hints at even the rudimentary usefulness of AI: as a helpful assistant to tweak your work in the right direction. Or to provide a starting draft. After my poetry experiment, I asked ChatGPT to come up with ten blog post ideas on the topic of content marketing. Again, half of the AI's suggestions were topics I'd written or thought about, and two suggestions were bad, but two were pretty good. I added those ideas to my editorial calendar. Then I experimented with asking ChatGPT to write a blog post for one of its better suggestions. The result? Not great prose, but it did meet a word count in under thirty seconds. Its writing was better than some non-writer humans I know, probably at the level of some of my C-grade first-semester writing students. In other words, with half an hour of editing, this copy would be presentable. Hmm.

A final anecdote brings the client into the picture. A month or two after my exploration and before a virtual meeting with one of my regular business clients, I fired up the old web browser to look at the client's company website and what was new on its socials. I glanced at the latest blog post and it really stopped my scroll — I was the company's blog writer, but this post was not written by me. It was written by … a C-grade first-semester writing student? Curious, I pasted the blog headline into ChatGPT and out came … parts of the post.

What was a writer to do? A frenzied interrogation and scolding of the client was out of the question, but so was ignoring it. Instead, I carefully raised the fact that I had noticed the post, and I asked where it came from. When the CEO hesitated, I asked if it was written by AI. He asked how I could tell. That's when I took the moment to educate him about the ways in which the post did address the topic posed by its headline but was full of generic and lifeless advice, not to mention awkward wording and overly lengthy sentences. If we were going to use AI, could we please pass it by the human writer/editor to punch it up a bit and make some reference to the company, maybe add some keywords? And instead of writing posts on random topics, we could stick to the editorial calendar we'd crafted with his audience in mind? He agreed.

But for me, this moment reinforced that change was going to happen with or without me. I needed to find ways to use these tools, possibly to prove the value of my humanity, and to expect that this reckoning would not be the last such incident. It could indeed be the future. For my part, since this client had opened that particular floodgate, I took the rest of the editorial calendar and asked the AI tool to write the first draft of all the posts remaining for the year. Then I edited the posts and punched them up and added company references so they sounded more like the company's house style. In a fraction of the time that it would have taken if I had started from a blank page, I had the next four months of posts. Hmm.

This is where I think that AI will have the biggest effect — giving writers (read: all professions) the time savings to let them move on to other work. For me, getting all my client's blog posts done in a quarter of the time meant that I could finally tackle the company's communications plan, which I'd had on the back burner for a few months. But this was a retainer client, where I was paid a flat fee and could move on to other projects. I had the same experience with another client later in the year when I used AI transcription to create and clean up captions for a series of videos (at this point I'm telling clients when I'm using AI for writing/editing tasks; I'm curious to see how AI acknowledgement will evolve). I had estimated a couple of hours per video, but AI transcribing the audio into words took a quarter of the time that I had expected, and I invoiced accordingly.

As a freelancer, this hurt a bit because I now had a hole in my schedule and an income gap on my spreadsheet. So, I think this is where freelancers may struggle: once AI has made our work easier (yay!) it may be challenging to find the volume of work we need to pay the rent (uh-oh). Also, certain client groups may choose to be satisfied with just the C-grade first-semester student version. Sometimes you can't compete with a budget of cheap (or free).

Editors face challenges but also have potential support from new tools. I often hear from non-writer friends about how they ask ChatGPT to improve their grammar or the variety of sentences in their writing. Of course, machine-based grammar correction has long been an option via other tools, and I would never wish Word's spell-check away, although I'm a bit suspicious of online tools like Grammarly, because there are often multiple ways to fix a sentence, and the machine does not always choose the best one, says this human. Yet I use tools myself to boost my editing skills; for example, PerfectIt is a plug-in for Word that helps verify consistencies in the document you're editing, such as whether you've spelled out acronyms on first use and abbreviated them subsequently. Yes, I could make a list of all the acronyms myself (and I do in my style sheet), but to have the tool identify and check them all automatically is a lot faster than my typing in each acronym. Just as we may be losing the client who uses AI to write a blog post and is satisfied with a more generic product, we may also lose clients who use AI to improve their own writing rather than hire an editor. Would they have hired an editor anyway? Probably not. But it's still a shift in the editorial space-time continuum.

At the same time, the fact that I was able to sidestep the tedium of transcription while still serving my client with fully accessible captions reminded me that I wouldn't want the progress to stop. When AI transcription came out a few years ago, I was an immediate convert. Transcription is the worst part of a writer's job

AI AND THE FUTURE OF FREELANCING

because it takes so long to listen to your interviews over and over to get to the point that you capture the quotes correctly — add up the five to seven thirty-minute interviews you might need for a feature article, and the total is many hours. I loathe it. I once tried to hire my mother upon her retirement and she lasted less than a day, so it's not just me. When AI transcription first came out, I paid $1 a minute to have the machines take care of it, which added up to over $3,000 that year (but I was able to write it off as a business expense, so that was fine). Even when transcription became affordable (dropping to $0.25 a minute, then to $0.10, then to free), I still had my students transcribe audio for their first assignment so they would feel the pain I had suffered early on in my career. I stopped that torture assignment after a couple of years when I realized I was being a mean luddite weirdo. All of this is to say that the time saved by this task (despite the need to correct AI transcription, which is still very unreliable) is something I will never give up, so while generative AI makes me uneasy, I know it is part of our future. Also, this is hardly the first time that a writer's life has been changed by technology (see: the internet).

Who said, "May you live in exciting times"? (Of course, as a writer I couldn't just leave this and looked it up — it was actually "May you live in *interesting* times," and according to Wikipedia it originated from a Chinese curse but is thought to be apocryphal. Not sure about that one. Hmm.)

Past Game Changers
Given my wish that this book have at least a bit of shelf life, I'm hesitant to write more about AI for fear it will be outdated by the time this book hits the shelves. Instead, I'm going to reflect on what has changed in the writing world, for freelancers in particular, over the span of my twenty-plus-year career, in hopes that this evolutionary record is the closest we can come to seeing the future.

Content mills were article production organizations popular around the 2010s for churning out large amounts of content, mostly blog posts, and notorious for paying very low rates. Companies bought these posts (and still do; they still exist) in the hopes that large amounts of keyworded content would help to increase their search engine optimization. For writers who were charging higher rates, there was a fear that content mills would consume a lot of work opportunities. There was also a sense that many content mills operated using offshore workers, something that was exploitive for their lower pay scale and also competed unfairly with North American creators. Yet another past-era phenomenon was the rise of pay-per-click articles, where writers got a (low) base rate and were then offered more money, but only if they got a high rate of readers clicking through. Again, we thought this could be the way of the future, but it's mostly faded.

Yet over time, the criticism of content mills was that the work they produced was low quality, somewhat similar to our current complaints about generative AI. My point is that they were a phenomenon that rose, frightened writers that they would soon be out of work, and now are no longer part of the daily chatter in writer circles. We survived them. Another example in the same vein are marketplaces where organizations can post their content needs and users can bid on the work. Fiverr is a worksite of this ilk, which originated along with companies like Elance (1998) and oDesk (2003), which merged and rebranded as Upwork in 2015.

Being a feisty freelancer, I'm always up for checking out such systems, and I tried signing up for Elance in its heyday but found it paid below what I needed to pay my rent. More recently, I signed up for Upwork; the wage range is quite vast, and I've met people who have made money on the platform. So that's proof there are ways to make money on such platforms; more to the point, there are different ways that content creation has evolved.

Industry Evolution

Besides content creation, content itself has changed. Starting my business in 2002, I recall when blogs were the hottest new thing. Now that makes me sound old. Wikipedia states that the term "weblog" was coined in 1997, and the earliest commercial blog took the form of an online diary by Ty, Inc. for its flagship product, Beanie Babies. By the late 1990s, blog usage had spread and tools were developed, with LiveJournal and Blogger among the first, in 1999. In 2005, *Fortune* magazine published the first list of top bloggers to watch. And by 2022, there were over 600 million blogs (en.wikipedia.org/wiki/Blog).

For a while, I felt like I was writing blogs that were really articles in disguise, then the rise of mommy bloggers in the 2010s, and travel bloggers, pushed the form. It took on an informal tone and included more visual elements. I feel like posts got short again for a while (does anyone remember 400-word posts?), then quite long. In Orbit Media's 2022 annual blogging survey, results from 1,016 bloggers showed that the typical blog length was 1,376 words, 70 percent longer than in 2014 (orbitmedia.com/blog/blogging-statistics/).

Search engine optimization (SEO), of course, was also a game-changer for blogs. Subheads and keywords went from optional to essential, and the search engines (they are like living creatures because you start to think of them as hungry little information goblins) began to prefer longer posts. With Queen Google regularly changing her algorithms, it's almost a certainty that the lengths and standards will change again. Maybe even before this book is published.

Perhaps even bigger than blogs has been the rise of social media. I recall in 2006 a friend who had just graduated from an American university telling me about this platform called Facebook that all her student friends were on and which was just starting to expand beyond campuses. Now we've watched that platform explode (then contract, then be vacated by the younger generation for other platforms, and then acquire the other platforms), the first of many. Some stick around for years, some don't (Rest In Peace, Vine), some come with a whole new playbook, while others riff on past forms (haven't newsletters been around forever?). For all of them, marketing types are challenged to come up with the best writing style to catch a reader's attention, forcing a continuous learning curve. Writing's not just about good grammar and sentence structure anymore. Although I'm as surprised as anybody that today's preferred medium seems to be text over voice, with even fewer Gen Zs willing to pick up the phone than Millennials, at least that's something for writers to celebrate. Smiley face winky face.

Now video is on the rise as a new way to consume writing, and any new writers should probably be trying to wrap their minds around scriptwriting and maybe even video editing. But if all of these adjustments feel a little exhausting, that's the challenge of an ever-changing business, and it's one that freelancers face possibly more than the traditionally employed because our standard answer to whether we handle a certain new type of content is often to say yes first and to learn how after.

In my job as the first dedicated online editor for the weekly *Saturday Night* magazine, I recall the struggle of trying to rally enthusiasm among print journalists to help me create a website and especially of finding original content to post there. This was in 2001, and no matter how many batches of cookies I ordered from catering for our weekly web meeting, attendance was scant, and, I'm afraid, journalists often attended only out of kindness to me rather than a true belief that the web was the future. In the years since, it's been interesting to see the role of online editor grow beyond an entry-level position and even to see many magazines flip to digital-first publication, with the print version a quaint legacy.

AI AND THE FUTURE OF FREELANCING

Part of the reason why the newspaper and publishing industry is struggling today is that most media owners did not embrace the shift to online and experiment more entrepreneurially with new advertising and subscription models that would help them pivot to what eventually became the standard of online readership. What reader is willing to abide by a paywall when they've been getting their content for free? Finally, in recent years, I've been encouraged to see new journalism projects emerging to experiment with how to keep writing and reporting alive. The podcast CANADALAND's reporting on the Canadian media landscape is a nice example. Like most media, we shouldn't expect journalism to die, but to change. Returning to AI, I know that my own world will change because of it; some of it will be great, like my transcription win, and some of it will be less great, like my worry that I will no longer be able to charge near the rate I did in the past for blog posts. For now, I'm still experimenting — and being transparent with clients about how I'm using AI — and still being a bit cautious about how I'm using it myself, since this technology is moving way faster than regulations regarding copyright or intellectual property.

If the writing platforms have changed at breakneck speed over these twenty years, their common goal of storytelling has stayed constant. I feel like I read the word "storytelling" more than ever today: everyone wants to proclaim themselves as a storyteller. Since we as writers are the original and ultimate born storytellers, our services will never be out of fashion, and the future, while changing, will remain bright.

THE FEISTY FREELANCER

© Iva Cheung

Conclusion

On Your Way

Throughout this book, I've tried to give you a sense of what the freelance lifestyle looks like, how it's worked well for me, and the shortcuts that can make it even better for you. As I have mentioned all along, I choose it for the lifestyle perks, the variety of work, and the sense of building something where my efforts regularly make a difference to my success — and because it's fun and every day is different. Whether you try freelancing part-time, full-time, for a long time, or for a short time, I hope you will feel the same. I'm not necessarily committed to freelancing forever (if the *New Yorker* calls, I'm out of here), but for most of my working life, it has grown to be my preferred way of work, to the point where what used to be "the job for now" is "the only job I want." Yay!

A final note if you do become a freelancer: remember that we are solo together — you don't need to just sit in your home office reading books about writing. Try joining your local chapter of a writers' association. Even better, volunteer — that's the way I met some of my closest writer/editor friends. Try taking a writing class to meet others. Make a plan to meet monthly over Zoom with other freelancers. Subscribe to magazines, buy books, support journalism and newsletter start-ups, and praise other writers and publishers for their efforts to keep this industry strong. And let me know how it's going by dropping me a note at feistyfreelancer.com, where I'll post extra Q&As, samples, and updates.

When you're working, keep in mind that what you agree to contributes to the industry. Don't sign bad contracts. Ask for a raise periodically. If you're feeling bored with your business, remember that you have the power to change it. Revisit your business plan annually to think about how you can keep building, whether it be to grow your income, find fun projects, take your dream vacations, or make time for an important hobby. Finally, make time for the occasional Friday afternoon matinee. Good luck!

Acknowledgements

Freelancing may be a solo journey, but it doesn't happen alone. We writer/editors need friends, family, colleagues, cat colleagues, and community to live a satisfying professional life. In my life, those people include my family, especially my mother, Sandra. You have always shown appropriate outrage when I call to commiserate about a bad contract and celebrated with me when things are going well. My brother, Bob, his partner, Nancy, and my feisty little niece, Lauren, are also among my cheerleaders, and I am always grateful for your support.

Thanks to my freelance friends, especially my Pitch Club pals, including Sharon Aschaiek, Sohini Bhattacharya, Carolyn Camilleri, and Jaclyn Law (meet them in the Q&A). You are great to travel with on this freelance journey. Thanks to my beta readers and friends Hazel Brewer and Susan Peters for your insightful comments on the first draft. To friends I've met through my association as a volunteer and in the community, I really appreciate knowing you and sharing information. Special thanks to the anonymous freelancers who answered my unscientific mini survey that added context beyond my own to topics like pricing and retirement.

Thanks to Dundurn Press for publishing this book, especially Kathryn Lane, who acquired it; Elena Radic, who shepherded it through production; and to my feisty editor, Robyn So, who worked on this book partly in Japan, where she was living her best freelance life visiting her daughter. Thanks to editor and editorial cartoonist Iva Cheung for letting me use her fantastic editorial cartoons in this book. Thanks to my chorus of freelancers for their advice in the Q&A, which helped me provide a wider perspective on freelancing while occasionally echoing and, therefore, bolstering my advice.

Thanks also to my editors and clients over the years and to anyone who has helped boost the careers of freelance writers. Thanks, finally, to my many students. You have helped me think through the elements that make up a satisfying freelance life. Your questions prompted me to write this book in the first place, and your fresh enthusiasm reminds me each term why I love being a writer!

Appendix A

Resources for Writers

Books on Writing
On Writing: A Memoir of the Craft, by Stephen King
On Writing Well: The Classic Guide to Writing Nonfiction, by William Zinsser
Bird by Bird: Some Instructions on Writing and Life, by Anne Lamott
The Spooky Art: Thoughts on Writing, by Norman Mailer
Six-Figure Freelancer: How to Find, Price and Manage Corporate Writing Assignments, by Paul Lima
The Wealthy Freelancer: 12 Secrets to a Great Income and an Enviable Lifestyle, by Steve Slaunwhite, Pete Savage, and Ed Gandia
How to Write Short: Word Craft for Fast Times, by Roy Peter Clark
Storycraft: The Complete Guide to Writing Narrative Nonfiction, by Jack Hart
The Bigger Picture: Elements of Feature Writing, edited by Ivor Shapiro
How to Write a Book Proposal, by Michael Larsen

Practical Guides
The Writer's Market
The Canadian Writers Market, 18th ed.

The Canadian Press Stylebook: A Guide for Writers and Editors, 19th ed.
The Canadian Press Caps and Spelling
The Chicago Manual of Style, 18th ed.
Editing Canadian English: A Guide for Editors, Writers, and Everyone Who Works with Words, 3rd ed., by Editors Association of Canada
Elements of Indigenous Style: A Guide for Writing by and About Indigenous Peoples, by Gregory Younging
The Elements of Style, by W. Strunk and E.B. White
The Conscious Style Guide, by Karen Yin

Podcasts
The Copywriter Club
The Writer's Co-op
Grammar Girl Quick and Dirty Tips for Better Writing
High Income Business Writing
Hot Copy

Writer/Editor Job Sites
Jeff Gaulin's Journalism Job Board — jeffgaulin.com
Masthead — mastheadonline.com
Quill and Quire — quillandquire.com/jobs
Work in Culture — workinculture.ca
Charity Village — charityvillage.com
Storyboard — thestoryboard.ca
Mediabistro — mediabistro.com
Superpath — superpath.co

Writer/Editor Associations
Editors Canada
Canadian Freelance Guild
International Association of Business Communicators (IABC)
The Writers' Union of Canada (TWUC)

RESOURCES FOR WRITERS

American Society of Journalists and Authors (ASJA)
Editorial Freelancers Association (EFA)
Society for Advancing Business Editing and Writing (SABEW)
American Copy Editors Society (a.k.a. ACES: The Society for Editing)
Canadian Association of Journalists (CAJ)
Chartered Institute of Editing and Proofreading (CIEP)

Appendix B

A Q&A Chorus of Other Voices

To broaden The Feisty Freelancer perspective, I interviewed a bunch of writers who are both careerists and occasional freelancers. These are their stories.

I'm also continuing this chorus through The Feisty Freelancer website (feistyfreelancer.com) and companion podcast — visit and tune in to read interviews with Margaret Webb, the late Krystyna Lagowski, longer interviews with each member of my Pitch Club, and more!

Feisty Freelancer Interview: Ann Douglas

Ann Douglas is an Ontario-based writer who specializes in parenting and is author of the Mother of All Books Series. Find her online at anndouglas.ca.

When did you start freelancing, and what kind of work do you do?
I started out writing for magazines and newspapers when I was in high school. We had a family cottage up in Muskoka, and another family on the same lake published a tiny community newspaper. They gave me my own book review column. I think I got paid $5 a column.

When I graduated university, I started sending out what we would recognize as official pitch letters. I worked for a community newspaper, and I quickly discovered that that was a bit too intense. As I started to have kids, I began to work for magazines, on a part-time basis. Initially I wrote for regional newspapers and magazines and then over time, I started pitching small "front of the book" pieces to places like *Canadian Living* and *Today's Parent*. Over time, I started to have the opportunity to write features for them. It built up gradually as time allowed and as I had a few clips.

You are a long-established voice in the parenting niche, and you're now moving into other areas like midlife and mental health. How did you choose and get started in your niche?
I have mainly been known for writing pregnancy and parenting books. At this point, I'm transitioning into wellness and mental health more generally because my kids are all in their twenties and thirties. So, I'm aging out of the parenting category, although I'm still really passionate about it, and I feel that parenting is a lifelong activity.

In terms of how that came about, in 1988 I gave birth to my first child, and suddenly I found that thing I had always wanted to write about. When my head started exploding with the challenges of parenting, I felt like I needed to write the book that I needed to read. For a long time, I wrote short articles and feature-length articles. Then in the late 1990s, I started sending out book proposals. I took a writing mentorship program through the Professional Writers Association of Canada, where I was mentored through the process of developing my first book proposal.

I got my book proposal out into the world. Once I had that first book published, a children's book called *Baby Science: How Babies Really Work*, then I was a proven commodity. I had shown to a publisher that I could do the work of actually delivering a manuscript. I could be out there on the publicity trail promoting it, because that is a huge part of the author's job. Then I kept sending out more book proposals and getting more books published. At this point, I've written and published twenty-six books. And that's not counting all the different editions.

What do you like best about freelancing?
Being my own boss. I don't think I would have done well as an employee in a corporation. If the rules were arbitrary and/or unfair, or I thought they were arbitrary and/or unfair, I would find it really frustrating. I think that's just the kind of personality I have.

Becoming a parent and deciding to work freelance has been a blessing for me because it allows me to choose what kind of work I want to do, who I want to work with, and to zero in on projects that are personally meaningful. If I don't get that sense of meaning, it's way too much work to do to write about something that you don't care about.

What are the challenges of freelancing?
I'm going to sound like an old grouch, but there are some things that really bug me. The lack of respect for what is actually involved in writing is at the top of my list. So many people think it's easy to be a writer or that everybody can do it. Being able to put text on a page isn't the same thing as being a skilled communications professional.

Then there's the fact that pay rates in our profession have actually declined over the course of my career. Freelancing is increasingly becoming a career that people do on the side while they work at a day job, or that only incredibly privileged people can afford to pursue. From a social justice perspective, that means we are missing out on the voices of so many of our fellow citizens. And that can be really damaging to the health of our communities and the strength and well-being of our democracy.

If we want Canadian creators to be able to afford to continue to do their jobs, then we really need to make sure that the pay rates being offered to them are being elevated. It's not okay that a dollar a word was the rate in the 1970s for many Canadian top-tier magazines and that today it's actually less. We really have a long way to go, and that is going to require writers banding together and working in solidarity.

What do you think is the solution? Is there anything else we writers can do?
A key thing is to compare notes with other writers. That way, you will know who is worth working for and who is not, because some publications may sound like they'd be great to work with, but maybe twenty revisions are required of your article as it gets passed around the desk, and you end up working for next to nothing. I think that we need to know who is worth it, who will forget to pay you, and to whom you may have to practically send a lawyer's letter to get paid. Because all of that bites into your productive time, and it can be really demoralizing.

How do you deal with the ups and downs of freelancing?
I think the biggest challenge for me is the ebb and flow of work. In hurricane season when I have a new book coming out, I'm sending out all kinds of emails and pitch emails to see if people want to review my book or invite me to speak at a conference. There literally aren't enough hours in the day to do everything.

So, I'll go through this sort of frenzied period. Then after the book has been out for a while, it'll start to slow down a little bit. I might even flirt with the idea of writing another book. So, it's very cyclical, and I think that sometimes we don't recognize the impact that these cycles can have on other people in our lives. When I'm writing a book, I'm very focused on the content and waking up in the middle of the night with the book running through my head. I can't imagine I'm a lot of fun to live with when I'm in that mode. Although, to be fair to my husband, when I was working on my most recent book, he announced spontaneously (and apparently without irony), "I love being married to a writer!" So, there's that.

As a long-time freelancer, how do you keep it interesting later in your career?
I love learning. I'm constantly challenging myself to learn new craft techniques and strategies. I take a lot of writing courses and participate in a lot of workshops. These days, I'm hard at work trying to teach myself how to write my first novel.

I'm also always re-examining things that I've written about in the past. And over time, I can see the nuances and reframe things in different ways. It's a compelling way to witness my growth as a person and a writer.

I'm never going to have time to write everything I want to write. So, I have to ask myself, "Where can I have my greatest impact?" I also have to consider what work has the greatest meaning for me personally. To me, success is not measured in royalty statements or dollars sitting in a bank account. It's more a matter of lives changed or lives touched in some way. I'm thinking of some of the conversations I've had over the years with readers who have said, "Your book helped me to get through a really dark and difficult time." Those kinds of conversations mean everything to me. In fact, they're the reason why I'm an author.

That doesn't mean that I don't want to be able to afford to buy new printer cartridges and all the other things that go along with running a business. I want and deserve to be paid well for my work. But I also think that in order not to completely burn out and collapse into a pit of cynicism and despair as a writer, you have to look at other measures of success than just how much money is sitting in your bank account.

What is the best advice you would have for new freelancers?
Connect with other writers. Writers need to be in community with other writers. They understand the joys and challenges of the writing life in a way that other people simply cannot. They can help you to figure out how the freelance writing business works: what it takes to succeed and how to pace yourself so that you don't burn out in the very first month. And they can share the recipe for freelance writing success: one part persistence and three parts self-compassion.

Feisty Freelancer Interview: David Hayes
David Hayes is an Ontario-based journalist, author, teacher, and ghostwriter. Find him online at davidhayes.ca.

When did you start freelancing, and what kind of work do you do?
I started my career in 1981. I had long-term career goals. I wanted to write for the biggest national magazines. And at some point, I wanted to make a transition to writing books. That seemed very far away in 1981, when I was just graduating from journalism school at Ryerson.

I started freelancing while I was in journalism school for very small papers and magazines, mainly writing about music. Music was an area that I was knowledgeable about and comfortable with, so it was the easiest way for me to break in.

Soon I started pitching things to the *Globe and Mail*'s weekend feature section. It paid around $200 for a 2,000-word feature. Even in those days, that wasn't much. Therefore, it didn't attract the top writers who were writing for the big magazines for a dollar a word. The editor started using me for long features that didn't even begin to pay for themselves. But the weekend *Globe* was very high profile.

I knew that it was being read by the editors of magazines, so that was a strategy meant to get me on their radar. And at the same time, I was eking out a living writing for small trades, little business magazines. Finally, I started writing short items for *Toronto Life* and *Saturday Night* magazines, and things grew from there.

In 1988, I started teaching part-time at Ryerson's journalism school (now Toronto Metropolitan University). Then I was hired on as full-time faculty in 1995. And stayed until 2001, when I left to go back into full-time freelance writing.

What made you go back into freelancing?
I wanted to keep writing. In 1983, I pitched a feature idea to *Saturday Night* magazine about a boy from Nova Scotia who had gone to visit his schoolmate in New Jersey and was involved in the double murder of the New Jersey boy's parents. He had been arrested and was serving twenty years in an American penitentiary. There was a feeling the Canadian boy had been railroaded and was much more innocent than the American boy. My editor, Gary Ross, said, "Why don't you pitch it as a book proposal; I'll help you edit it."

So, I wrote a book proposal, he edited it, and I sent it to five publishers. To my surprise, all of them were interested. So, on the strength of that, I was able to acquire a literary agent, and I've had one ever since. The book was published in 1986. I thought it would be another five or six years before I would be able to do another book, but a second book followed in 1992, and then a third two years later. I ghostwrote my first book in 1996 and began doing a lot of ghostwriting in the 2000s. That's the whole career in a nutshell. Maybe you can distill it into three sentences.

How did you find clients throughout your freelance career?
Pre-internet, marketing was word of mouth. In fact, I would argue that today, word of mouth is just as important. I mean, sure — I'm on

LinkedIn, I have a website, I use Facebook. But basically, I still think that your reputation and word-of-mouth stuff is the most important.

Some of my work comes from my literary agent. She's always trying to find ghostwriting projects for me. But back at the very beginning, other than business cards, really the only marketing you had was people you knew. You start working for a publication with an editor who likes you and continues using you. And meanwhile you're pitching to another magazine and another magazine. And pretty soon, one of those editors will say to another editor, "David Hayes is a pretty good writer." Suddenly you get an assignment from some editor you've never heard of. That still happens today, but there are so many fewer publications and editors now.

Today, you really have to market yourself. Blogs are extremely good. If you do a good, targeted blog about the subject area or areas that you are most interested in writing about, that can be useful. Now there are umpteen ways a freelancer can market their brand.

What do you like best about freelancing, and what are the challenges?

Freedom and flexibility. If I have to go shopping, I can do it anytime. If I have to go to Ikea, or to a big grocery store, I can go on Tuesday morning when Ikea is almost empty. As a freelancer, I never go anywhere near an Ikea on a Saturday or Sunday. I can work at night; I can take the morning off. I love the flexibility.

People would say the challenges are that you wouldn't work at all. In fact, I find people who are self-employed, working out of their home as I do, sometimes work longer hours than people I know who have a nine-to-five job. I frequently work on the weekend. But I might work over a whole weekend because I have a lot of work and then that means I take Tuesday and Wednesday off. I go to a movie on Wednesday afternoon at three o'clock. I can't remember when I last went to see a movie at a mainstream movie theatre on a Friday night. I mean, why would I want to go? It's crowded, people are talking. I go at times when the theatre is three-quarters empty.

What questions should people ask themselves to figure out if freelancing is right for them?
Are you able to motivate yourself to work? Almost everybody who hasn't done it thinks they couldn't possibly motivate themselves. So, ask yourself, "Do I really want to do it?" If the answer is yes, then try it, at least for a short time. Because I think, in fact, most people could do it, as so many people found out during Covid or if they found themselves out of a job because of downsizing. They're just afraid to. I'm sure there are people who would find it too stressful. But most of the people I know who are freelancers, and that's many different kinds of people, have adjusted to it. If anything, you almost work too much, because your office is right there in your home. I sometimes close my office door to remind myself that I've stopped working.

Any final advice for freelancers?
This is a long game, and you have to think of it that way. It's not about how successful you become next week, or how many successful things happen in six months. You're gradually learning more, honing your skills as a writer, researcher, and interviewer, making contacts, and your business slowly builds. If you're frustrated and feel discouraged after one year, then you're probably not suited to being a freelance writer, because it isn't measured that way.

Feisty Freelancer Interview: Paul Lima

Paul Lima is a long-time, Ontario-based technology and business writer, teacher, and trainer and the author of many freelance writing e-books. Find him online at paullima.com.

THE FEISTY FREELANCER

When did you start freelancing, and how did you begin?
I've been a freelance writer and business writing trainer for about thirty years. I started writing for newspapers and magazines and then transitioned into writing for companies. I also provide training in business writing and promotional writing. Now I have moved from conducting workshops to doing webinars.

I'm an English major from York University. I have a copywriting background. I was working full-time as a copywriter, and I taught continuing education courses. I have always supplemented my writing with corporate training. Teaching continuing education courses helped open doors to training for me.

Working as a copywriter, I learned how to write to deadline, how to write concisely, and how to write in a punchy manner. I think copywriting made me a stronger writer. And that helped me with my journalism. I think most journalists move from journalism to promotional writing. I went the other way. And then years later, I moved back into copywriting, as a freelancer.

How did you decide on your niche in technology and business writing?
I looked at myself and asked, "What do I know? Tech. So I could write for tech companies?" Those were my first clients. I'm a firm believer in focus, so I would pitch tech companies. But as you start writing for clients, once you've written a white paper, you're thinking, *Okay, who else could I write this for?* Maybe financial institutions. Like, I would never write for, say, health services. I know nothing about health services. You look at yourself, your education, your work experience, and you say, "Who can I sell my services to, based on who I am?"

When I started to freelance, it made sense that I would write about technology as it relates to business. Some of that became a gold mine for me. I wrote about technology and business, and that led to writing strictly about business. There is an evolution if you want there to be. I didn't have to evolve, but I started to see doors opening and opportunities.

How did you find clients and market yourself?
Well, the way any freelancer gets a client, you pitch. It's the only way. I suppose you can go to events and meet editors in person and chat them up. But they'll still want an idea from you. They'll want an article idea and to see samples of your work.

If you live in a house, have a wife and a child and a car and a dog, you think, "How am I going to make a living? I have to learn how to market my services." So, cold calling, emails, phone calls. Once you've written several times for a client, and they've paid you, then you want to make sure you follow up with them. As freelancers, we have the same marketing tools that major corporations have. I'm not suggesting that you buy ads on TV, but you can market yourself in similar ways that any business can: generate repeat business, get testimonials and referrals, do cold calling, cold emailing, set up a website, put samples of your work on the website.

How do you find story ideas?
ABC — always be curious. I would walk my dog and meet people and be talking to them. You run a telescope retail company? I think I could pitch an article idea to the *Toronto Star* on what you're doing. You make buckets out of wood not using any nails? I think I can write about that. I think there's an article on how dogs enable you to socialize, and I pitched that to the *National Post*. They replied within forty-eight hours. So, it's just always be curious. What are you interested in? What are you passionate about? There are article ideas in that.

What do you like best about freelancing? And what do you think are some of the challenges?
Like many writers, I'm an introvert. So, what I like best about it is I get to stay home and not see people. I don't mind solitude is what I'm saying. I don't mind working on my own, and I don't mind trying to generate business. I like, in fact, the solitude of working on my own and being responsible for making my own income.

The challenges are similar to what I like best. Marketing is a challenge. Meeting your deadlines can be a challenge. You need to be disciplined. Producing good copy is a challenge. I think most freelancers will tell you their biggest challenge is making a living. I've been very successful for a long time. But I've worked damn hard at it. I've worked evenings and weekends, and I wake up, have breakfast, and turn on my computer. I think the biggest failing of most people who can write and who don't make much money at it is a lack of discipline. They don't know what to do, so they don't do it. Or they know what to do, but they don't schedule the tasks.

How do you think freelancing has changed over the years?
I think it's harder to make a living as a freelance journalist, because publications are going under or cutting back. So that hurts. But the buggy whip–makers, you know, when the automobiles came along, they stopped making buggy whips. You have to adapt or you die. So, if you want to make a full-time living at freelancing, I do think you need to do more corporate work. At the same time, there are freelance journalists who are still making a living doing journalism.

You also have written several e-books, which are very useful resources for other writers. What motivated you?
As a freelance writer, you soon notice that things really start to slow down from early- to mid-December to about mid-January, because people who are working full-time are on Christmas holidays. So,

every year I would have six weeks with not a heck of a lot to do. And I don't mind putting my feet up, but one day, I'm teaching this course and I'm having difficulty finding a really good textbook. So, I wrote the textbook. Then the next year was, like, so what else could I write?

What questions should people ask themselves to find out if freelancing is right for them?
I think what most people don't understand is the discipline required to run your own business. Never mind be a freelance writer, to run any business. That is what's often missing. And to be a disciplined person, you have to know what to do. So, you have to understand the business end of being a freelancer. And then you have to be disciplined in terms of how you approach the work. Pitch, pitch, pitch; write, write, write. That's all there is to this.

Any final advice for freelancers?
Pitch and write, write and pitch. Be disciplined in your approach. Also, if you're writing for corporate clients, and somebody approaches you through your website, and they're a small business that you've never heard of before, take an advance or even payment in full before you start to write. I'm not saying that they're going to rip you off, but there are some businesses that will rip you off.

Learn a little bit about marketing, a lot about writing, and a little bit about accounting and the business side. It's not rocket science; it's not brain surgery; this can be learned. If you are struggling with the writing, and yet you love to write, take a course. Don't shy away from education.

Feisty Freelancer Interview: Heidi Turner

Heidi Turner is a long-time freelance writer based in B.C. and the creator of the Happy Freelancing newsletter. Find her newsletter online at happyfreelancing.substack.com.

When did you start freelancing, and what kind of work do you do?
I've been freelancing full-time since 2006. I went to an information session for a program that was run at Douglas College called Print Futures. I honestly thought they were going to teach me how to write the great Canadian novel. I came out of that session with all this information on communications and public relations and writing jobs. So, I decided to take the program. I was able to take some freelancing courses in, like, running a business and finding clients by marketing yourself. I realized that seemed like what I really wanted to do. When I ended the program, I was working as an office manager at a plumbing company, and I started taking on clients, and one day I just realized it was time for me to take the jump into freelancing. Two or three months after I graduated, I decided to go in fully.

How did you choose your niche?
I always loved the law. I had thought about going into law; I actually took the LSATs. And then I realized it wasn't for me — writing was more my thing. When I came out of the program, there was actually a job advertised for writing for an online legal marketing agency. They wanted a freelance writer, and I met with the woman who was the editor. She liked my experience, my knowledge of the law. So that led me to my first niche, and I stayed writing mostly about law for probably ten years. Then lately, I've started to transition into financial writing.

How do you find clients and market yourself?
I have a lot of clients who have reached out to me on LinkedIn who become long-term recurring clients, which is fantastic. And either they found me directly on LinkedIn or they've met with someone I'm connected to who has referred me. But aside from that, a lot of my work is referral or word of mouth. People hearing about me or clients recommending me to people that they know.

A Q&A CHORUS OF OTHER VOICES

What do you like best about freelancing, and what are some of the challenges?
What I love about freelancing is you can constantly reinvent yourself. A lot of freelancers tend to get stuck at the start of their careers because they think that whatever they choose now, they have to stick with forever. And you don't. Actually, you have a lot of freedom to change your mind. You don't have a boss looking down telling you that you have to be this certain thing for your whole career. I also love that your career trajectory isn't set in stone. You can stay like a small, one-person business for the rest of your career, if you want. You can do it as a sideline forever. Or you can branch out and run your own agency, or work as a freelancer for a while and maybe do a part-time in-house position. You have a lot of opportunities and variety in how your career can look.

Probably the frustrating thing most freelancers will say, it's the ebb and flow of income. You can have an amazing month where you are making five figures, and then all of a sudden, something happens. Clients lower their priorities, or they change their project focus, and you're scrambling again. So, trying to find a balance or even that out over the long term can be very challenging. And it can be disheartening.

What do you do when you find yourself in the ebb instead of the flow?
Unfortunately, a lot of the things that you do involve being proactive, so building up an emergency savings account, where you have a few months of bills set aside, so that you're not panicking right away. And constantly be marketing yourself. Don't stop connecting with people. Find time, at least every week, if not every day, to be reaching out, getting your name out there, and engaging in conversations. Someone might not be ready to work with you today,

but all of a sudden, in four months they'll have a ton of work for you because everything has piled up.

Can you reflect on how freelancing, and maybe even writing itself, has changed over the years that you've been in business?
It's changed so much. When I started, obviously the internet was a thing, but I don't know that there was really terminology like content marketing; it was just sort of all copywriting. I think it's great that there are different avenues that freelancers can go into, whether they want to do a lot of marketing writing and audience lead generation or they want to do more informative writing.

Also, social media has changed everything. You can market yourself now to clients around the world. I work for agencies in the U.S., one agency that has a head office in the U.K., and with writers in Australia and editors around the world. That's really opened up the door for a lot of different careers. One of the jobs that I'm becoming known for is localization, where I'm taking copy that's been written by an Australian writer for a U.S. website and making it applicable to a Canadian audience. So new careers have popped up.

Do you find any difference in freelancing in B.C. rather than in Toronto, where there is a higher media concentration?
That's an interesting question; I don't know that I've ever really thought about it. The only time I found it really challenging is in coordinating meetings. Because what I have found is that the expectation is that I will get up earlier, not that people will work later. So sometimes that becomes a bit of an issue. Less so now, I think, because of Covid. More people have gotten used to having to adjust their working hours or be more available for meetings. But in terms of my work, I don't know that it's really affected too much, because so many of my clients are from the States or are from Australia or New Zealand or the U.K.

You and I met when volunteering with writers' associations. What do you like about participating in writing communities?
It's so great. A lot of us get into freelancing partly because we don't want to deal with office politics. We want to work on our own, we might be a bit introverted. But that can also lead to a bit of tunnel vision. Joining a writers' association, number one, it makes you not feel alone. You're part of a community. By going and sharing, if something's frustrating you, if you're going through a tough time, you have people to talk with about that. But you can also see what's possible, you're surrounded by people who are successful. And you can share their guidance and their wisdom, what lessons they've learned. You can see that even if something is tough for you right now, there is a way through it. That's really important for your mindset when you go into freelancing.

What are some tips you have for freelancers starting out?
It sounds obvious, but it's not: you have to take your business seriously. It can be very easy, when you can work your own hours, work in your pyjamas, get up when you want to, to view your business as an afterthought. That also sometimes happens when we view ourselves solely as freelancers and not as business owners. Then we don't market ourselves the way we should, we don't start reaching out. I think that regardless of why you get into freelancing, if you want to be successful, and you want to be in it for the long term, you have to take it seriously as a business.

Feisty Freelancer Interview: Steve Slaunwhite
Steve Slaunwhite is a long-time, Ontario-based copywriter, prolific trainer and teacher, and a co-author of *The Wealthy Freelancer*, among other books. Find him online at steveslaunwhite.com.

When did you start freelancing, and what kind of work do you do?
I started freelancing in the mid-1990s, mostly local businesses, mostly print. I started part-time as a side hustle, but I had every intention that I eventually would go full-time. It took about three years before I felt competent enough with the money I was making each month. And I've been freelancing since that time, full-time without a break.

Halfway through my last twenty years, I guess from 2004, I started doing copywriting workshops and training. Right now, about half of my business comes from doing copywriting and content writing workshops. And then, the other half is writing for companies.

How do you get clients, and how do you recommend new freelancers start finding clients?
A lot of my work is referrals and word of mouth. But what I tell new freelancers is there is a client out there right now today who has a project that they need your help on. And they would hire you in a moment. The only problem is they don't know you exist. So, a big part of marketing yourself as a freelancer is prospecting.

Prospecting is letting people know what you do, introducing yourself and your services to people who are likely to be potential clients. Let them know you exist. And if you do that with five hundred prospects, you're going to get some action. And you can prospect in many different ways. Networking at events, email prospecting. LinkedIn is a great place to connect with people and introduce yourself and services. Whatever you're comfortable with, there's many different ways.

What do you like best about freelancing?
What attracted me to freelance writing was that I saw it as a ticket to realize my dream, which wasn't necessarily of being a writer — it

was of being self-employed. Back in the 1990s, there was this whole work-at-home movement. Everybody wanted to work from home. So, my dream was to be self-employed and work at home. I had a background in creative writing, and I also had a sales career at the time. I figured that I could combine the two, and that became copywriting.

What are some of the challenges you've found over the years?
I know a lot of people say that the challenges come with the ebb and flow of getting clients and making money, the lean times. I have to admit, I've never really felt that too much.

That doesn't mean I've always been successful. I mean, I've had many nights where I've woken up at three o'clock in the morning and started mentally doing calculations in my head, going, "Okay, I'm working on this project that's worth $3,000. I have another client coming down the road. That project might come in that might make enough for me." Every freelancer worries about money because it's up to you to make the money. I've always worried about that, but I've been lucky in that I've never gone broke.

Also, I find deadlines are a challenge, getting things done. Because I'm a solo professional, it's up to me to get things done. If a project doesn't get done, I don't get to invoice. So, the stakes are high.

But something I really like to emphasize when I talk to other freelancers is that you need to take care of yourself financially. Because you don't have a pension, you don't have employment insurance. You need to put money in the bank and keep it there. You need to put away your retirement savings. No one else is going to do that for you. And you don't want to end up being sixty-five and not having taken care of yourself financially.

Do you have a retirement plan?
Oh yeah. I squirrel money away in RRSP savings and stuff like that as best I can. I'm not perfect, but I've done pretty well. One

thing that's really helped me is that from the start, I paid myself a regular paycheque every two weeks. I pay it to my wife. It's always the same amount. Although I've given myself raises over the years, obviously.

But that has instilled some discipline in my business because I have to make my payroll. I'm very proud to say that since I began, I've never missed a paycheque. It's on an automatic deposit even.

How do you think freelancing has changed over the years?
The internet changed everything. When I started in the 1990s, I was at the tail end of those years where everything was print. There weren't that many copywriters around. I worked mainly with local companies. Then the internet came along and two things happened.

Number one, you could suddenly work with clients anywhere. You work with clients all over North America, across the world. Also, companies now needed websites and emails and all of this online stuff. And then later on, blogs and social media. The amount of stuff that companies need written has tripled or quadrupled. And your ability to work with anybody in the world, so your market, your potential pool of clients, is the world.

Now, there's a downside with that. It's easier to hang a shingle and call yourself a writer. There's a lot of competition these days. I think the biggest difference is in positioning and differentiation.

You also train other copywriters now. What inspired you to start that?
I wrote a book around 2000 for Self-Counsel Press called *Start and Run a Copywriting Business*. I always wanted to write a book. And because of that book, I started to get the occasional invitation to speak. I'm not a natural public speaker, so it was really a stretch for me, but I found that I started to really enjoy it. I enjoyed the teaching. So gradually I've gotten into doing more workshops, creating courses.

And one thing led to another. I teach copywriting at the University of Toronto; I do a lot of teaching for American Writers and Artists Institute (AWAI). And I do corporate training as well, usually for marketing teams or sales teams.

As a long-time freelancer, how do you keep it interesting? Do you find that this training has added something to your overall career?
It spices it up a little bit. It allows me to do some interesting things. Although you have to be careful. If you're a freelancer, you have to be careful about going off in too many directions. Even if all those directions are interesting, it's very easy to become overwhelmed, and you're diluting your efforts. I've experienced that myself. I've gone off in many different directions all at once and ended up with an identity crisis. Who am I? What do I actually do?

Any other advice for newcomers to freelancing?
The most important advice I would give to a freelancer starting up is to realize that it's going to take a lot of hard work and determination to get your freelance business off the ground. To set things up, figure out how you're going to prospect and market yourself, hustle and go after clients. And finally, land that first client or gig, and then land your second one, and start making money.

Feisty Freelancer Interview: Rob Marsh
Rob Marsh is a U.S.-based copywriter and co-founder of the popular podcast the Copywriter Club, which is online at thecopywriterclub.com.

When did you start freelancing, and what kind of work do you do?
I started freelancing when I started my career. My very first project was in 1993. And then I used that to leverage myself into an

in-house gig. I was in-house for fifteen to twenty years, and I did freelancing on the side. I came back to freelancing in 2014, after I had sold off a company that I was running. I was thinking what I really love doing is copywriting. At that point, I had a lot of contacts in the marketing world. So, I just started reaching out to people, saying "This is the person I help. This is the problem I solve."

How did you decide on your niche?
When I was writing in-house and in agencies, I didn't really have a niche. I worked on all kinds of different products: medical, home security, pets; it was just this mad variety. But throughout my career, I spent a lot of time doing two or three different things. A big chunk of my career was writing for a company that specialized in health and vitamin supplements. And then another chunk was spent working for tech companies or SaaS [software as a service]. Now I've niched by deliverable, and mostly what I write is sales pages. Occasionally, I'll add in abandoned cart sequences and some of the emails that go along with sales pages, but I love writing sales pages.

How do you find clients, and how do you market yourself?
This has changed over the course of my career. When I first started out, I actually reached out to just about everybody that I knew in my network. I basically spent a ton of time, not cold pitching, because I knew these people, but warm prospecting, reaching out to people who knew what I could do because we had worked with each other before.

At some point, though, you exhaust that level of connections, so at the same time, I was working on building up my authority in the various spaces. Posting in places like Twitter or LinkedIn, trying to build that. At the same time, I also launched the Copywriter Club, and that has done a ton to build my authority and have people see me as an expert in the space. So today, most of the work that I get is through referral or from somebody who will see me answering a question somewhere.

While we're on the subject of your very successful podcast and mastermind empire called the Copywriter Club, of which I am an alumna, why did you decide to start this community, and why do you think it is helpful for writers?
We started the Copywriter Club because we wanted a community that would feel helpful for the kinds of writers that we were engaging with. My co-founder, Kira Hug, and I were in several other groups. Most didn't feel all that helpful. If somebody asked a beginner question, you could get all kinds of comments about being a newbie. Some people just weren't that kind about people who really wanted to learn and engage and listen. So, we thought, let's start something that is welcoming to everybody: experts as well as beginners. I think it resonated with people and grew.

I wish that I had engaged with communities and masterminds and other copywriters sooner than I had — I tried doing it on my own forever. Had I had peers or mentors in my back pocket, instead of trying to figure it all out myself, I would have made a ton more progress. That's why I think communities are so critical.

How do you think freelancing has changed over the years?
I don't know that marketing or sales has changed that much. What's changed is the opportunities to market ourselves and the various platforms where we can do it. Thirty years ago, you would market yourself at a networking meeting in person. There was no internet.

Now, you go on any of the social media platforms. On LinkedIn, there's a ton of copywriters and content writers talking about the things that they do — same on Instagram and in Facebook groups.

The number of opportunities where we can share our expertise has blossomed. That's the biggest thing that has changed. What hasn't changed is that you need to be an expert, you need to talk about the things that you do, you need to solve problems in public.

What do you like best about freelancing? And what are some of the challenges?
Everybody will talk about the freedom. And you know, it is nice that I am not required to drive to an office. If I don't show up exactly at eight o'clock in the morning, there's not a boss there to get mad at me. I can take time off. But that's also the negative, right? Because when we are our own bosses, sometimes we're a little permissive in the amount of time that we allow ourselves. So, the downside is that I've got a pretty good boss who lets me take time off. Also, I've got a pretty bad boss, who sometimes encourages me to take off more time than I should. You have to have a level of discipline to make this work.

What are your top two or three tips for beginner freelancers?
My number one tip is, if you are a writer, you write every day. Even if you don't have clients, you need to be writing for yourself, creating samples of the work that you want to do. If you want to write blog posts, and you don't yet have a client, write ten blog posts for yourself, or identify what kinds of clients you want to work with, and write ten blog posts that they might look at.

Number two, you need to find a client. Finding a client to work for is more important than getting your website perfect. Or making sure that you're saying the right things on social media. What I said about how I found my first clients is the exact same advice that I would give: figure out who it is that you help, and then go out and tell everybody that that is the person you help. And when I say everybody, I mean, tell your parents, your grandparents, your cousins, former work colleagues, friends, former bosses. That is the level of dedication that you need to have to spread the word.

Any advice for senior freelancers who might have been doing it for a while and want to keep their business interesting?
That's a great question, because senior freelancers hopefully have got a lot of things figured out; they've got the systems that are working for them. They've got a skill set; they've demonstrated that they're good at solving those particular problems. They're good writers. And so, my advice is, okay, what can you do to grow? Whether it's growing your skills, working with better clients? Or what is it you want to achieve in your life? Maybe it's working with higher-paying clients or finding a different niche or something that allows us to have more time for other things. Explore or play around with anything that you want to change or do differently.

Feisty Freelancer Interview: Sandy Yong

Sandy Yong is an Ontario-based freelance personal finance writer and author of *The Money Master*. Find her online at sandyyong.com.

When did you start freelancing, and what kind of work do you do?
I started my freelance writing journey after I had published my book, called *The Money Master*, which is a personal finance book teaching Millennials how they can invest in the stock market, real estate, and also start their own business. This was February 2020, right before the pandemic. So, when the whole world shut down, I really had to think about what I wanted to do in order to grow my business.

I started to network within the industry and build relationships; things started to align. My first opportunity was to be a monthly columnist with *MoneySense*. I had my own column, called "Making

It," where I would educate Gen Z on how they can navigate being an adult. From there, things naturally snowballed: I was able to get more clients, especially in the personal finance and investing space. It's been nearly three years or so, and now I'm pursuing my freelance writing and speaking business full-time.

How did you choose your niche?
In January 2018, my husband was thinking about a New Year's resolution, and his goal was to write a book. We were part of Toastmasters, a global organization to help individuals develop their communication, public speaking, and leadership skills. We noticed that our friends who had decided to pursue a speaking business full-time had actually written their own books, which provides a lot of credibility and increases authority. We ended up going to a book writing seminar in Toronto with our now book publisher, and that really opened my eyes to learning how to build a business. When I was trying to figure out what kind of book I would write, that's when I realized that I have this passion for personal finance. I had created a successful six-figure investment portfolio in the stock market as a self-directed investor.

How do you find clients, and how do you market yourself?
One of the ways has been through networking. People take me on as a freelance writer, and I provide really high-quality work, and I make sure that I meet all the deadlines. I'm easy to work with, and I have a lot of positive experiences and feedback from my clients. From there, it's been a lot of word of mouth. Editors tend to be connected with other editors, and whenever they're looking to hire freelance writers, they'll bring up my name.

Another avenue is through LinkedIn. I keep my LinkedIn profile up to date. With my portfolio, usually I'll put in a weekly social media post, just to share the work I'm doing. And then lastly, using platforms such as Contently, or ClearVoice, that connect clients with freelance writers.

What do you like best about freelancing, and what are some of the challenges?
Freelance writing gives me an opportunity to be creative with my writing. I get to write about topics that I'm passionate about and get paid for it. It also provides me with a flexible work schedule. In the past, I was juggling a corporate nine-to-five job. With freelance writing, I was able to work on my assignments during the evenings or weekends. I'm able to keep learning and growing my business, which has been very rewarding.

Challenges I face would be that sometimes I can be my own worst critic. What helps is that I will talk about my feelings or my experiences with my husband, and he will give me pep talks or help bring perspective to a situation. Also, with being a freelance writer, there is a feast or famine cycle, so the work can be unpredictable. The landscape is always changing, and you have to be strong-minded and know that the quality of work that you provide is good enough. I've come to a point where I have developed a client base and I get recurring work, so I just have to remind myself that things will work out.

You self-identified as a millennial; do you find any challenges as a younger writer?
One of the ways for me to keep connected in the industry is I'm part of an organization called the Canadian Freelance Guild. There are definitely more seasoned freelance writers in that group. The advantage is that I get to learn from their experience and expertise, because some of them do have decades of experience. They often tell me stories of how it was back then, even like in the '80s or '90s. And how magazine or print publications used to pay much more than

they do now. It's very interesting to see how things have changed so much in the past few decades.

Do you have any advice for new writers?
I would say build your client base and keep track of how much you're earning on a monthly basis. Doing that over, say, a year or two, you can see your trajectory and how your business is doing. Because in the beginning phases, it can be very volatile or unpredictable. But over time, as you get more clients and increase your fees gradually, then you can forecast how you will do.

Also, to have a business plan, to really know what your niche is, who you're writing for. The more you niche down, the better. If you're a generic writer and you're trying to cater to everyone, then you're really not catering to anyone. You want to be top of mind when people are looking to hire you.

As author of *The Money Master*, what financial advice would you have for freelance writers?
When you start building your business and you start getting serious money, stay organized. Make sure you keep all your receipts and have an Excel spreadsheet to keep track of your income and expenses. Take the time to understand that you're following the rules when it comes to tax season, because you don't want the CRA to come after you and start questioning. Set aside between 20 to 30 percent of your income, especially if you are collecting GST or HST for your business. And don't spend that money, because you are collecting the taxes on behalf of the government. Keep it in a separate account where you're not tempted to spend that money.

Reinvest that money that you earn into yourself, whether it's education or taking courses to improve your skills. That way you are improving on your freelance writing, your expertise. Whether it's reading books or attending conferences or events or webinars, I think that it's a good way to network, expand your industry connections and those relationships, because you never know where those connections will lead.

Feisty Freelancer Interview: Susan Peters

Susan Peters is a Manitoba-based writer who has freelanced full-time as well as worked in-house as an editor and is now in corporate communications. Susan was a helpful beta reader for *The Feisty Freelancer*!

When did you start freelancing, and what kind of work do you do?
I freelanced a little bit when I was in my twenties, and then I worked as an editor full-time for a number of years. I freelanced full-time for about ten years before returning to an office in a corporate communications role. When I was young and freelancing part-time, I was just sending out pitches to magazines and online publications. I had a full-time job as a newspaper editor and as a magazine editor.

I liked to write magazine articles, and I pitched national Canadian magazines. And I also did a lot of work for businesses and non-profit organizations. I've written blog posts for businesses, proofread for corporations, and written articles, brochures, and press releases.

What did you like best about freelancing, and what do you think are some of the challenges?
What I liked best was the diversity of the work — you're working with different clients on different projects all the time. Even if a project is not the most interesting thing in the world, in a month, you'll be doing something different.

One thing that made me switch into a full-time job is that as a freelancer, you don't get a promotion when you've been working for a number of years. There's no such thing as a senior freelancer, you won't have a pre-determined course for your career. You would have to create your own opportunities, and if you look around at friends' careers, you can see them getting more senior roles. I wanted those options.

I also found it isolating to work from home, and I was looking to work in a team environment. Another drawback of being a freelancer is being a hired gun, working at an arm's length. You might not know what changes are made to a project that you've contributed to or what changes have been implemented after you've turned work in.

How do you think freelancing has changed over the years?
Writing freelance articles only for magazines has become a less viable business because the pay rates haven't gone up much, there are fewer magazines, and there's just generally less money there. So, when I was freelancing full-time, I branched out into writing for businesses, and I liked that and I'm good at it. I thought of it as helping people to solve problems.

You live in Winnipeg, Manitoba. What kind of clients can you pursue in Winnipeg? Also, did you write stories about the area?
I had corporate clients and small-business clients in Winnipeg. Most of those came to me through word of mouth. I worked with a design agency and partnered with them on a few projects.

When I was freelancing, I thought a lot about regional stories that I could pitch to national publications that wouldn't otherwise know about stories happening in a region. A good story from a region would be a local story that has national implications. A great example in Manitoba would be stories involving the town of Churchill, because it's an important arctic port for shipping, scientific research, and also it's a popular tourist destination.

Did editors like hearing from you as a writer from a smaller centre?
There's definitely an interest in having writers in smaller centres who are able to pitch and who are able to pitch local stories. But I would tell writers in non-large and major centres, don't just pitch local-angled stories. Pitch national stories. Don't limit yourself. There's only going to be a small market for stories in national magazines from Red Deer. But if you can pitch a national story and write it from Red Deer, then do it. If you only pitch stories that are based in your local region, that's limiting yourself. You're not going to make any money, and you're not going to publish that many articles.

You're an editor as well as a writer. Do you prefer one over the other?
I like the variety of doing both. I've always thought of writing and editing as two sides of the same coin; they are related skills. What you learn as an editor helps you to become a better writer and vice versa. When I was a newspaper editor and I had interns who wanted to be copy editors, I would make them write an article first and have the experience of having their work edited, so they could understand what it feels like to have someone make changes to their work.

What is your best advice for newcomers to freelancing?
I was more of a generalist freelancer, and I loved the variety, but for other people, it's also good to be a specialist and focus on a niche. Keep yourself organized in your work; I write to-do lists on paper, and they freak people out because they're quite long.

Also give yourself a raise occasionally. I had a long-term client that I did editing for on an hourly rate, and one thing I started to do is raise my rate at the start of every year. I set a percentage, usually reflecting inflation. I would send the client an email announcing what the new hourly rate would be, effective as of January 1 of the new year. I felt glad I did that. Otherwise, I would have been working for them for 10 years without a raise.

Feisty Freelancer Interview: Laura Berg
Laura Berg is an Ontario-based social media entrepreneur, author, and teacher who is online at lauraberginc.com.

When did you start freelancing, and what kind of work do you do?
I work with entrepreneurs to create their YouTube channels. With my YouTube channel, I work with brands as an influencer.

When I first started, it was a means to an end. I was a teacher, and after I had my daughter, I wanted to stay at home with her. And I had to make money. I had a background in sign language, and I signed with her. One of my friends said, "Why don't you teach other parents how to sign with their babies?" So, I started a business called My Smart Hands (mysmarthands.com), where I ran baby sign language classes out of my living room. Then I had people start emailing me asking if they could be an instructor with my program. So, I took the opportunity to create a program. I always call myself an accidental entrepreneur, seizing opportunity.

So, then I thought, what's the next thing that I can do? One of the things I started doing was teaching other entrepreneurs how to use YouTube to grow their brands. I got certified with Google as a YouTube audience development specialist. Then I started a website that says that I help entrepreneurs to learn YouTube, and then I sat back and waited for people to contact me.

And now I do content for brands. Brands will approach me, and I'll come up with an idea. They have a concept of what they want. For example, we worked with Kumon. They said they wanted content that showed a love of learning beyond the classroom. Working as an influencer, I set it up that way.

What do you offer as an influencer, and how do people work with you?

I have a management company that deals with my YouTube channel, so all of the brand deals come in through them, and they want to work with me for access to my audience. It's usually companies that want to reach families, parents of young children. They will have a concept, and then I have to come up with an idea of how to put that video together. I come up with the idea, they approve it, and then I produce the content. All the content that I produce on my channel for a brand also has to fit into my brand. I don't want to just do a commercial; I want to do something that would be interesting for my audience.

Typically, clients come to me for video. I have done blog posts. A lot of times it's a campaign, so you have a video, and then you have to have social posts to support the campaign. The past few campaigns I've done have just been exclusively on Instagram. So, it depends on the medium.

How has your business evolved?

Originally, it was just me and the baby signing world. And the mommy-blogger world. And then I started becoming interested in the idea of entrepreneurship and growing a brand using social media. Back in the day, before social media, small companies were not able to grow the way that they can now because of access to the digital world. To me, that's fascinating; I love that. So that's how I've grown, through my interest in that. I've learned more and more about the digital world and entrepreneurship and marketing. I've moved a bit away from the baby-signing world as my children have grown. Now I'm really passionate about the marketing and digital business world.

How has YouTube and social media changed over the years? Are they good tools for freelancers?
I started on YouTube, just after it launched. It was really, really early days. So, I've kind of grown with YouTube. But now it's very saturated. It is very hard for somebody to get on and become an influencer. But that's not to say it doesn't happen. I think that it's a really fantastic way to promote yourself or your business. They say that video is the way of the future and where marketing dollars are going. Because people want video — people want information through a visual medium.

What do you like best about freelancing, and what are the challenges?
The thing I love the most is the freedom, just being able to do what I want to do. When my kids were little, I volunteered on every single school trip, I went to every play, and we'd go on vacation at times of year that weren't peak time. I just love that I don't have to ask permission. If I want to go to the spa and have a massage on a Wednesday afternoon, I do that. If I want to meet a girlfriend for lunch and have a glass of wine and sit for two hours, I can.

Challenges — oh, there are many. I mean, especially in the early days, it is so hard to get started, to actually get that momentum going. Like pushing a rock up a hill. And you can see the top of the hill where you want to get to. But getting there, that's so much work. Once you're there, it's so much easier. I think the biggest challenge is the isolation, being alone and not having somebody to bounce ideas off, which is why I always tell people that they should get a brain trust of other entrepreneurs.

What kind of advice would you give to somebody who is looking to be an influencer?
I think a lot of people are so concerned with the numbers and the followers that they have, whereas brands are now realizing that it's not the numbers that matter. It's more and more micro-influencers that they're looking at, which are smaller influencers who actually have more influence than the bigger influencers, because of their engagement. So, I would say, concentrate more on building a community and having that engagement versus having big numbers. Because as a brand, if you have, say, one thousand followers, but when you post something, five hundred of those people comment and like it, versus somebody who has one hundred thousand followers and only twenty people comment, it's more about the comments and likes. It's more about the community and the engagement — that's what brands are looking for now. So, starting out, look to be a more micro influencer and a niche influencer.

Also, avoid taking anything and everything that comes your way if it's not really authentic to your brand voice or to what your audience would want. Just understand your worth from the beginning. Be able to communicate that to whomever you're working for. That goes for any freelancer. That's the hardest part I think, determining your worth and asking for that. I think a lot of freelancers undersell themselves.

Feisty Freelancer Interview: Iva Cheung

Iva Cheung is a B.C.-based freelance editor and editorial cartoonist who is online at ivacheung.com. She contributed her editorial cartoons to this book.

When did you start freelancing, and what kind of work do you do?
I started freelancing part-time when I was in grad school. I was finishing up a physics program and transitioning into a publishing program.

During that time, I edited some peer-reviewed articles and books in the physical sciences, because that's what I was familiar with. After my publishing program, I worked in-house for a few years. The second phase of my freelancing began after I left that position and ramped up the freelancing to pretty much full-time. That was back in 2011.

How did you choose your niche?
I worked at a non-fiction trade publishing house. That's what I continue to do: I edit trade non-fiction, academic books, and reports for non-profits. I have two main niches, if you want to call them that. I tend to gravitate toward, number one, cookbooks, because I love food and cooking, and cookbooks tend to be very beautifully designed. I love being in that world. My second niche, which is probably the bulk of my businesses, is plain language. I gravitated toward plain language because it has such a clear equity and accessibility angle, which I find very motivating. I think we all deserve to understand the information that we need to make important decisions that affect our lives.

Why is plain language important, and is it in demand as an editorial skill?
Most of the clients that I work with on plain language projects are typically non-profits or academics who want to make their research more accessible. For example, I might work with health authorities or health communication organizations that want to make sure that their information is clear.

Plain language does have an official definition; it comes from the International Plain Language Federation. They say that communication is in plain language if your intended audience can easily find what they need, understand what they find, and use what they find to meet their needs. This applies to not only the words but also the structure of the document and the design.

Cookbook editing sounds fun too. Do you go and make the recipes?

These last few years, I've actually been more specialized in cookbook indexing. It's super fun for me because at that point, the book is pretty much done. I'm compiling ingredients and recipe names so that people can find the recipes they need. But I also do copy editing for cookbooks. And that really is about making sure that the ingredients and the method match up, that the measurements make sense. We don't necessarily test every single recipe, but intuitively we should know that a whole kilogram of cilantro is a little bit much, and that would be a point to query. I bring this up as an example because there was recently a book that I worked on that called for an entire kilogram of cilantro.

Do you identify as a freelancer? How do you find clients and market yourself?

This is probably the toughest question for me to answer because, yes, I am a business owner. But socio-politically, I also consider myself an anti-capitalist. So being an anti-capitalist business owner has a fair share of challenges. I'm not comfortable marketing myself at all. But the way I go about it is to try to find and build community. This really took the shape of my volunteering for organizations like Editors Canada, both at the national and local branch levels. I like to meet people and then also document the professional development that I'm doing and sharing what I learned. That took the shape of blog posts. I think people in the editing community got to know me that way, and so I've been super fortunate that by doing that I have built a network of fellow freelancers. We refer work to one another. If something comes across my desk that doesn't suit what I do, but I know somebody else who is in that niche, I'll pass it along to them. That's primarily how I've built my business and my client base.

What do you like best about freelancing, and what are some of the challenges?

I love the flexibility in terms of how I can schedule my day. And the variety of projects that I can work on is also really motivating. When you're working in-house, sometimes you get assigned to projects, and you don't necessarily get to choose. Choosing as a freelancer is also quite a privilege. I do appreciate the ability to say no to clients who might not be philosophically aligned with me. In those cases, I just know that I'm not going to be a good fit. And so, I'm not going to give them my best work. In terms of the challenges, certainly the feast and famine cycle is super real at both extremes, and they're stressful for different reasons. And my least-favourite activity has got to be chasing after invoices.

How has freelancing changed over the years you've been in business?

I think the pandemic had a big effect on the way I have been able to build relationships with fellow editors. Here in B.C., we have Editors BC [a branch of Editors Canada], and we have monthly meetings. During the pandemic, and afterward, we moved all of our monthly meetings online, which is fantastic; I absolutely think that it's the way to go for accessibility reasons. It means that people outside of the Lower Mainland of B.C. or Metro Vancouver can participate in these meetings. At the same time, though, it's also meant fewer opportunities to get together in person and just chit-chat about what folks are working on, get to know new editors who want to start their own businesses, or get to know what people are interested in editing so that you can refer folks and build those relationships.

And then, of course, there's different technologies emerging that might have an effect on what we do. Whether you think large language model, AI stuff, is going to hurt or hinder writing or editing, it's certainly going to have an effect. In this period of uncertainty, not knowing what that's ultimately going to look like, how much we should invest in learning them, and how much downward pressure they might have on rates. For example, people who don't necessarily understand what we do might ask us to edit something that was generated by AI. And there's a lot of very sticky ethical and legal issues that haven't been fully resolved yet.

What is some of the best advice that you've received from other freelancers?
This is also a tricky question, because a lot of the advice I'm still struggling to implement myself. I guess the most important is to try to avoid devaluing your own work. For me, this is a huge struggle because, again, I'm an anti-capitalist business owner. So, I just have to bear in mind that if I undercharge, I'm not just harming myself; I'm harming other freelancers. Because we set expectations among clients about the value of our work. Another good piece of advice that I sometimes don't implement is to track our time — even if we're charging a project-based fee — to get a good metric for how we're using our time and whether the project was better or worse value than other kinds of payment arrangements.

What tips would you have for freelance editors starting out?
Try to find your community. We are independent contractors, but we're part of an interdependent ecosystem. I would not be able to do this alone. You need friends and colleagues to bounce ideas off, to do gut checks with, and to refer work. You need a community of people you can trust. Find your community, whether that's online or by participating in organizations like Editors Canada, Editors BC. I'm a member of the Indexing Society of Canada as well and Plain Language Association International, PLAIN Canada.

The second tip is to never stop learning. There are always opportunities to get better at what you do and to bring more value to your clients. Learning doesn't all have to come from formal sessions, like webinars or courses. You can learn from anybody, in any kind of setting. And along the same vein be super generous with your referrals and with your knowledge. It has been very important for me to really value my relationships with other editors and other people in publishing, and to see them not as competitors but as allies.

Feisty Freelancer Interview: Allison Finnamore

Allison Finnamore is a New Brunswick–based freelance writer and president of the Canadian Farm Writers' Federation. Find her online in partnership with writer Trudy Kelly Forsythe at cultivatingcommunications.ca.

When did you start freelancing, and what kind of work did you do when starting out?
I've been freelancing since 1991. I was trying to get closer to where my then fiancé was living; I heard about a freelance opportunity at one of the weekly or daily newspapers in New Brunswick. So, I did that for about a year and then switched to one of the other daily newspapers and did that for twelve years.

Do you think of yourself as being in business?
I was always freelancing for the newspapers. But at some point, I remember thinking, "Okay, I'm not a freelancer anymore. I'm a business. I write." That was a change in mindset. It was almost like growing up. All of a sudden, I felt like people were taking me more seriously. Maybe it was just in my own head. I was taking myself more seriously.

How did you choose your niche in farm writing?
When I was working in Woodstock, New Brunswick, for the daily newspapers, freelancing, I was young and eager and had no children, and I was working my tail off. I was writing probably an average of fifteen stories a week, everything from murder trials to town council meetings. And since it was a farming area, I was writing about potatoes. Potatoes started to become a regular part of my beat. Then I had a call from an editor of a farming publication in Nova Scotia. And she asked me to go to a cattle breeders' meeting. I knew nothing about agriculture. But making that connection with that editor planted the seed that maybe I just don't have to freelance for the daily paper.

In 2001, my husband and I moved from Woodstock to Moncton, New Brunswick. We had a toddler, I was pregnant with my second child, and I took that time to get settled. I was doing this stay-at-home mom thing, but by the time spring rolled around, I was anxious to get going and do something else. I was a member of PWAC [Professional Writers Association of Canada] at the time. And we had a meeting at my house, the kids were down for a nap, and we went through Paul Lima's *Six-Figure Freelancer* book page by page. We did the workshop right at my kitchen table. And part of that is finding your niche. I thought, *well, there's this agriculture thing*, and there was no one in Atlantic Canada writing about agriculture for the Western publications. I thought, *you know, we've got some pretty good stories to tell*. My kids were little, but I didn't want to be working full-time, so I was making those inroads as I could and building my business at the same time as I was building my knowledge.

Fast forward to today and now you are fully a specialist in agriculture. What does your business look like?
My main client is a corporate client I've been with maybe fifteen years. I was a contributor for three or four years and then moved

into the role of editor. There are two publications that I edit, and that involves managing the budget and finding the freelancers and that sort of stuff.

We met through the former Professional Writers Association of Canada, and you now volunteer in new places. So do I. How has volunteering benefitted your career?
When I started with PWAC, I had just started working. I was twenty-two or twenty-three. At that time, I had no idea how to write an invoice. PWAC taught me that business side: how to pitch, how to invoice, how to follow through, all of those really core business skills. I'm heavily volunteering right now as the president of the Canadian Farm Writers' Federation. And I'm involved with the Atlantic Canada Farm Writers' Federation, and we're hosting our annual national conference in Nova Scotia in October. At the Canadian Farm Writers' Federation, our conferences are made up of tours of farms, so we spent one day on the bus, and then one day in professional development sessions. I've toured farms, in the last twenty years, all over the country. And I've met hundreds of farmers. That really gave me that that background and that fundamental knowledge in order to write about agriculture for an agricultural audience.

Also, at the Canadian Farm Writers' conference, you're not going to find anyone who stands up at the front of the room and says, "Hey, I'm looking for freelancers." But if you're there, and you're working and talking to people and meeting everyone, and you're passing out your contact information and letting it be known that you're there and you're looking for work, then you will get those callbacks and it will pay off. There are always opportunities; you just sort of have to be open to them and put it out there that you're open to them.

What do you like best about freelancing, and what are some of the challenges?
I like the flexibility. I'm at my cottage, and I've got my Wi-Fi, I've got my laptop. If I want to get up at 4 a.m. and work for a few hours and then walk down to the beach, I can do that. I mean, it's a give and take, so sometimes you're working on projects, and you're up at 4 a.m., and you're still working at 8 p.m. But if you want to take a week off, that's fine too. Things like pitching and finding the work, that's work. If you don't have the work, then your effort needs to be in finding the work. Money management is also a challenge because it ebbs and flows.

How do you think freelancing has changed over the years?
Anything that I say will make me sound old. But certainly, the whole social media thing. Just having that presence, that's an investment in your time. Promotion of yourself and getting out there and getting known; you need to be doing those things constantly.

The best interviews are in person, and since the pandemic, we're more tempted to go to Zoom or Teams or whatever first, and those in-person stories, they're getting lost a little bit if we just default to online meetings. I miss that one-on-one connection; I think that's where the magic happens. It's when you get to actually sit down with someone.

Do you find any difference in freelancing from New Brunswick rather than in Toronto, where there is a higher media concentration?
I don't know, because I've always lived in New Brunswick, so I don't have much to compare to, but I do have a friend who is a member of our farm writers' organization; she's from Nova Scotia and she went to university in Guelph. She's often talked about how we're just at a slower pace here, so there isn't always that urgency or that maybe

the sense of competitiveness is not as sharp. One time I wrote a story about backyard garden trends, and I interviewed someone from one of the universities in Nova Scotia, and he said that the gardening trends that are happening in Toronto will happen in Atlantic Canada in ten years.

What advice would you have today for younger freelancers starting out?
Get involved with whatever organization, whether it's Editors Canada, or the Canadian Freelance Guild, or niche organizations. I get a little frustrated sometimes by the "what can your organization do for me," so flip that, like, how can you contribute? Groups are always looking for volunteers. And then when you're always putting it out there that you are available for work, maybe you'll be the first person to come to mind. I have a friend who will, whenever he has a change in his clientele, put on Facebook, "I have capacity right now to take on new clients, so if you're interested, give me a shout." Sometimes we're a little bit shy to promote ourselves. If you're using the social media channels, then be blunt and put that out there and sell yourself.

Feisty Freelancer Lightning Round!
A few quick answers from the (in)famous Pitch Club who help keep the feisty in Feisty Freelancer.

Thanks to my freelancer friends who joined in my Pitch Club and have been a great support throughout my personal freelance journey over the past few years. Now meet a representative sample: higher education writer Sharon Aschaiek, real estate writer Sohini Bhattacharya, writer and magazine editor Carolyn Camilleri, and long-time freelancer-turned-*MoneySense*-managing-editor, Jaclyn Law.

When did you start freelancing, and what kind of work do you do?

SHARON: I started freelancing full-time in 2004. My business is called Higher Ed Communications, and I provide writing, editing, communication advising, and publication management services to universities, colleges, and other organizations connected to the higher education space. Storytelling is the main part and biggest joy of my work. I do a lot of article writing for alumni publications, newsletters, blogs, annual reports, and other communication vehicles.

SOHINI: I started freelancing back in 2013. I was working in a PR firm for a few years, and my work involved a lot of writing, copywriting, communications materials, newsletters, press releases, brochures, and articles and pitches. When working at the PR firm, I realized that I was not getting to do as much writing as I wanted to, because a lot of the work was also about event management. And that was something that I was not into at all. Writing is what I really wanted to do more and more of. So that's when I quit the PR firm.

And the day after I quit, I started building my own business as a freelance writer. I really pushed myself out of my comfort zone socially and started networking like crazy, looking up organizations where people work with freelance writers. It pretty much grew from then. The work that I would look for was as a copywriter, as a ghostwriter, as a grant and proposal writer, and from there I also branched out a little into journalism, so I could write for my passion projects.

CAROLYN: I started freelancing casually in 1996, first as a proofreader and copy editor while I learned about magazine design and production. When the company I was working for went under in 1998, I officially set up my freelance business and continued to focus on custom magazines for various organizations. The work involved budgets, promotional/sales materials, planning, research, editorial lineups, writing, copy editing, layout, proofreading, and publishing. I was very fortunate to work with a team of highly experienced and creative people. We later went on to launch several other publications, including some very successful in-house magazines.

I still work with that team on their custom publications, but when I moved to Toronto in 2013 [from B.C.], I branched out to include writing and editing for other clients, mostly for magazines, articles, websites, blogs, and reports.

JACLYN: I started freelancing when I was in high school, writing paid articles for the teen magazine where I'd done a co-op placement in grade 12. After finishing university, I started working in magazines, first as a research assistant and copy editor at *Chatelaine*, and then as managing editor at *Abilities*. I kept freelancing on the side, earning a little more each year but not taking it very seriously — I considered the income "vacation money." I was laid off in 2006, and that's when I decided to try freelance writing and editing full-time. I was fortunate to find clients quickly. At first, I worked mainly for magazines, but over the next fifteen years, my clients gradually shifted from media to corporate, where the money and work are more plentiful. I love freelancing, and I didn't think I'd ever go back to a salaried job, but never say never — two years ago, I got an amazing opportunity at a magazine I've long admired: managing editor of *MoneySense*. So that's what I'm doing now, with just a bit of freelancing on the side.

What do you like best about freelancing, and what are the challenges?

SHARON: What I enjoy most about freelancing is the freedom to shape how, where, and with whom I work. I decide which projects and clients to take on, and I organize my workdays around my other life priorities. I can work as little or as much as I'd like according to my goals and ambitions. Having control over work-life balance is deeply important.

The biggest challenge is navigating the ebbs and flows of freelancing with grace. When work is quiet, I have to remind myself that this is part of the natural cycle of self-employment and to use the downtime for business development, marketing, and administration. Also, working for myself can be isolating, so I've cultivated routines to keep me engaged with my professional community — for example, by attending professional development and networking events and being a part of a writers' club.

SOHINI: I love the flexibility. As a freelancer, I could choose my own hours, I could work from where I wanted. I could go out and sit in the backyard and work from there. I could sit in a coffee shop. You call the shots, to choose whether you want to work on long-term projects or short projects, and you can take vacations when you want to and work on vacation or not.

Some of the other things that I really like about being a freelancer are I can select my own projects, the kind of clients I want to work with, and what industry I want to write for. For example, I did love writing for real estate. So, I gave myself that opportunity to grow and develop myself as a real estate writer, learning about the trade and how dynamic it is and how it fluctuates from one year to the next.

In terms of challenges, I feel like we're constantly hustling. I don't like hustling. I like to be able to know that I can rely on certain types of clients. It's like dating, right? You keep looking, and finding the right client is like finding gold. The uncertainty of income is one more thing. It can be a feast or famine kind of career, for those starting out. Sometimes you are flooded with work. And then sometimes you'll have these dry patches. You use the dry spells to work on building your business, but you're aware that you're not getting any money for it. So, that can be a bit of a motivation killer.

CAROLYN: What I love best about freelancing is that every project is different in some small or large way. Whether it is a full magazine, website, or article, the subject matter and clients are different. There are always goals to meet, challenges to overcome, and things to learn. People are passionate about what they do, and that energy is contagious and makes work very interesting and exciting.

The challenges with freelancing are the same as ever: knowing what to charge, making enough money, finding clients, and staying current in everything from technology to terminology to audience.

Keeping your courage up and believing in your own value can sometimes be the biggest challenge. A comment from another writer or editor, someone else's success, and even tiny things like hesitation over comma placement or word usage can make you wonder whether you've made the right career decision. I remember having something akin to an identity crisis when the label "content strategist" entered the field. Even the most successful freelancers have times of doubt, stress, and even fear — don't be too hard on yourself.

JACLYN: My favourite thing about freelancing: flexible hours and scheduling. It's really nice to have the freedom to book appointments, get personal stuff done, and take time off when you want to or need to, no permission required. As for the challenges of freelancing, my top three are (1) working too much — when you run your own business, you can end up working all the time to the detriment of other things in your life (like exercise and socializing). I know, it can be hard to turn down work. It often feels like leaving money on the table. But recognize that there are only so many hours in the day and only one of you. Overbooking yourself only lessens the quality of your work; (2) slow-paying clients — most clients do pay in the end, but it's time-consuming to have to follow up on unpaid invoices multiple times; (3) procrastination — like every human, I sometimes put off tasks I don't like or enjoy. Deadlines are great motivators!

What tips would you offer someone who wants to be a successful freelancer?

SHARON: Be involved in your local communities for writers and communicators. Connecting with other freelancers is vital to staying in the loop on industry trends, learning about new work opportunities, collaborating on projects, and having people to turn to for advice and moral support. It's also useful to build ties with complementary professionals, such as editors, graphic designers, project managers, and photographers, as they can also help you connect with work leads.

Always be marketing. Whether it's by attending professional development or networking events, blogging, speaking, buying ads on LinkedIn, publishing a newsletter, or maintaining an up-to-date SEO-optimized website, it's important to be regularly maintaining and building your business presence and engaging with current and prospective clients. This is key to learning about and being considered for work opportunities.

Consider developing a niche. You will have an advantage in the market if you can specialize in a particular type of communication or writing service, e.g., a product like case studies or annual reports; an audience, such as donors or employees; or a sector, such as health care, IT, or finance. The more you can distinguish yourself as a writer, the more you will stay top of mind with clients and prospects. As you further develop as an expert in your chosen domain, you'll be able to command more money for your services.

SOHINI: My first tip is to find your niche. Find what you want to specialize in. Don't try to be everything to everyone. Second one, and this is not something that I did very well, is building your social and online platforms. In today's world, unfortunately, these are really the places where your business needs to shine for people to notice your work and for clients to look for you. Third, know what you're worth, know what your work is worth. Set your rates and if anyone questions it, know how to defend your rights as a freelancer and stick to your rates.

CAROLYN: Be flexible and open-minded about work opportunities and your business plan. Freelancing is truly a voyage of discovery, not only in finding projects to work on but also in learning new ways to work in a constantly changing world. You may have interests and strengths you don't know you have yet that could lead you in all kinds of wonderful directions.

Join groups. Talk to people. Learn from others. And don't focus only on writers and editors — get to know designers, photographers, social media people, sales people, funders, and the people who are reading or using the materials you are creating or want to create. Learning more about what other people are doing and what they need broadens your perspective, gets your name out there, and may lead to collaborative opportunities.

JACLYN: Do a great job, finish on time, be professional, and be pleasant to work with. That includes following directions, anticipating needs, communicating effectively, and welcoming feedback. Also, negotiate fair rates, keep upgrading your skills, network with other freelancers, and manage the financial details of your business, including billing, expenses, taxes, and insurance. It's a lot, but you've got this!

Index

accountant. *See under* taxes
agencies, 114, 199
articles, 87
    fact checking, 100, 128
    how to write, 87
    interviewing, 91
    journalism jargon, 99
    planning, 89
    revising, 98, 126
    story ideas, 64
    structuring, 97
    workback schedules, 89
    writing, 95
artificial intelligence, 206
assignment letters. *See under* clients

benefits. *See* business start-up
branding. *See under* marketing
burnout. *See under* productivity
business start-up, 45
    benefits, health, 39
    business name registration, 45
    business plan, 41
    domain name registration, 49

insurance, health, 39
insurance, professional liability, 60
tools and technology, 57

clients, 119
    assignment letters, 120
    handling feedback, 125
    process of approvals, 129
    working with, 122
contracts, 152
    copyright, 153
    indemnification clauses, 156
    moral rights, 156
copy editing. *See* editing: stages
corporate work, 103
    letter of introduction (LOI), 110
    pitching corporate clients, 103
    prospecting letter sample, 111
    researching corporate clients, 107

editing
    niches, 28

pricing, 146
stages, 26
estimating. *See under* pricing your work

freelancing
    challenges, 14
    client mix, 115
    common tasks, 12
    day in the life, 19, 187
    definition, 11
    generalist vs. specialist, 28
    niches, 31
    perks, 13
    schedules, 19, 134, 187

goal setting, 34
    creative and personal, 38
    financial, 35
    retirement planning, 40

home office. *See* working from home

insurance. *See under* business start-up
invoicing. *See under* payment

jargon, industry. *See* articles: journalism jargon

magazines, 68
marketing, 165
    branding, 177
    networking, 170
    referrals, 176
    social media, 169
    testimonials, 176
    websites, 167
masthead, 68

editorial titles, 68
matinees, afternoon, 1, 5, 35, 43, 185, 216
mindset issues
    impostor syndrome, 24
    perfectionism, 136
    writer's block, 135

networking. *See under* marketing
next steps for freelancers, 193
niches. *See under* freelancing
non-profit work. *See* corporate work

payment, 158
    getting paid, 161
    invoice sample, 160
    invoicing, 158
    pricing services, 143
    tracking payment, 162
pitching, 75
    format, 78
    process, 82
    sample, 79
pricing your work, 143
    approaches, 143
    by the word, 146
    estimating, 150
    rates, 144, 146
    surveys, 147
productivity, 133
    batching, 137
    burnout, 140
    pomodoro, 137
    taking breaks, 184
    virtual assistant, 138
proofreading. *See* editing: stages
prospecting letter. *See under* corporate work
publications. *See* magazines

INDEX

query letter. *See* pitching

reading like a writer, 63
referrals. *See under* marketing
resources, 219
    reference books and style guides, 59, 219
    writer/editor associations, 171, 220
retirement. *See under* goal setting

samples
    interviewee email, 92
    pitch, 79
    prospecting letter, 111
self-employment. *See* freelancing
social media. *See under* marketing
story ideas. *See under* articles

taxes, 51
    accountant, 55
    collecting tax, 51
    filing, 56
    write-offs, 54
teaching, 200
testimonials. *See under* marketing
time management. *See* productivity
tools and technology, 57

websites. *See under* marketing
workback schedules. *See under* articles
working from home, 179
    dressing up, 184
    finding a space, 180
    structuring your day, 182
    taking breaks, 184
writer's block. *See under* mindset issues

writing
    forms, 24
    niches, 31
    pricing, 144

About the Author

Suzanne (Sue) Bowness has been a full-time freelancer since 2002. She has written for many publications, including the *Globe and Mail* and *University Affairs*, and on topics including education, careers, business, technology, and books. Her business, CodeWord Communications (codeword.ca), specializes in strategizing and creating long-form content.

Since 2004, Suzanne has taught writing courses at various colleges and universities. In 2012, she earned a Ph.D. in English from the University of Ottawa, with a dissertation on nineteenth-century Canadian magazines. In 2015, Suzanne helped to develop and launch Humber College's Professional Writing and Communications graduate certificate. Suzanne has been a long-time volunteer with Editors Canada and the Professional Writers Association of Canada. She has won a National Magazine Award B2B (Silver) and two Canadian Council for the Advancement of Education awards.

Suzanne is also a creative writer with a published book of poetry, *The Days You've Spent*, and other works-in-progress.